)

BOB RIPLEY

LIFE *beyond* BELIEF

A PREACHER'S DECONVERSION

Foreword by
Rev. Dr. Daniel Meeter
Old First Reformed Church
Brooklyn N.Y.

Binea Press

Published in 2014 by
Binea Press, Inc.
512-1673 Richmond Street
London, Ontario, Canada N6G 2N3

Tel: 519.660.6424
E-mail: binea@rogers.com
www.bineapress.com

Distributed by:
Binea Press Inc.
519.660.6424

Library and Archives Canada Cataloguing in Publication

Ripley, Bob, 1952-, author
Life beyond belief : a preacher's deconversion / Bob Ripley.
Includes index.

ISBN 978-0-9881323-6-8 (bound)

1. Title.

PS8585.I558L53 2014   C813'.54   C2014-904698-7

18 17 16 15 14   1 2 3 4 5

Design by Amanda Boltë
London, Ontario, Canada
Tel: 519.697.7977

Printed in Canada by Friesens Corporation
Altona, Manitoba

The invisible and the non-existent look very much alike.

Huang Po

For D.K.L.

· FOREWORD ·

Imagine St. Paul in reverse, undoing his conversion, getting back up on his iconic horse, and making a U-turn on the Damascus road. He's not a Christian anymore. He's not St. Paul anymore, he's back to being Saul of Tarsus. He's been un-born-again. Only he's not returning to Jerusalem; he's not going back to his native Judaism. You could say he's been born-again-again, and this time to atheism. He's not going back to persecuting or punishing or imprisoning. So he'll take the turn-off that leads to Tarsus. He's going to rest a bit, and collect his thoughts, and then he will set down to write.

He'll write a Second Epistle to the Romans, and Second Ephesians, and Second Colossians, with all the passion and fervor of argument he wrote his first epistles with: "I was wrong, we were wrong, we Jews were wrong, we Christians were wrong, and even the Greeks are wrong. There are no gods, there is no god, and that guy who was Jesus of Nazareth—well, that's all he was, a guy." This is the image that came to me half-way through my reading of this book by one of my best friends.

I've known Bob Ripley for twenty years, and we've gotten very close. For most of that time we've shared our Christian faith. We love each other and trust each other. I was one of the first persons he told that he was doubting the faith and thought he'd have to resign his ministry. I listened and sympathized as Bob related to me the arguments against believing, the arguments which follow in this book.

It doesn't matter that these are not new arguments. It doesn't matter that very many people have struggled with these arguments, and answered them, and still come out believers. Even if you don't find these arguments convincing they are compelling. None of you have the privilege to dismiss them out of hand. You can't side-step them or avoid them. Those horrible commands of

God are in the Bible. Those gospel details are contradictory. The blood-guilt of the church is undeniable. These problems will not go away, and Christians have to answer them.

I've spent years dealing with these issues, reading science, philosophy, and theology, wrestling with texts of terror and asking what good the whole thing is. I've come though it as a believer, a joyful one, and I confess the historic Creeds without crossing my fingers. But this book would have value to me even if I did not love the author, because this book expresses the ordinary, decent, candid, and questioning mind of most of the people who live around my church in Brooklyn. It's their unbelief, not my belief, which is the norm and the default. I'm the one who has something to prove, not them. It would be a great mistake for a Christian to take offense at anything in this book. If anything, this is where you have to start. So if you're a Christian, you should take this book seriously, and if you're not, well then you'll find companionship.

Underneath the questions which Bob is raising in this book is lots of passion and emotion. Just like with St. Paul. You will feel frustration, impatience, annoyance, and anger. Just like with St. Paul. The more I read St. Paul the more love I feel in him, for which I think he doesn't get enough credit. There is love in this book too. It takes love to open yourself like this, to make yourself so vulnerable, to do the work, to plead your case, to bear witness to the hope that is in you.

Bob Ripley did not have to write this book. He could have just let it be. For years he bore witness, and he still bears witness. For years he hosted the testimonies of others, and now he's giving one himself. He's telling the truth as he sees it. He believes that this is one of the most important things we human creatures owe each other in this passing life. I do too. He would invite you to do the same, and give you the space to do it in. I invite you to give that same space to him.

Rev. Dr. Daniel James Meeter
Pastor, Old First Reformed Church of Brooklyn, NY.

· TABLE OF CONTENTS ·

· EPISTLE TO THE READER ·

The pilgrimage from religion to reason has been mainly private and oftimes painful. My running coach John Ferguson says that when the Marathon gets tough just put one foot in front of the other. So I must begin by thanking those who, when the run was rough, unknowingly encouraged me to put one foot in front of the other along this path.

I begin with the late and much lamented Christopher Hitchens. Reading his strident rhetoric was initially a shock to the system but I'm grateful that he had the courage to write what I'd been thinking for some time.

I'm indebted to comedian Julia Sweeney who reminded me that we can let go of God one step at a time; to philosophy professors Dan Dennett, Victor Stenger and A. C. Grayling for making thoughtful cases against religion in favour of science and reason; to Bart Ehrman whose Biblical scholarship led me to take Holy Writ more seriously than ever before; to astrophysicist Neil DeGrasse Tyson and biologist Richard Dawkins whose enthusiasm for learning how we all got here in the first place has made me want to learn all I can about science, a subject I once scorned in favour of the arts.

Now to those who have directly encouraged me. The first person I confided in was my long time colleague and friend Dr. Daniel Meeter who writes the Foreword for this book. His response was that whether I was a believer or not, he still loved me. Thanks Dan. You will always be the Scarecrow but you are also the Tin Man by virtue of your heart.

My thanks to Professor Randal Graham who has encouraged me to tell my story and offered invaluable guidance as the manuscript slowly took shape. To paraphrase Dorothy Gale, you're the best friend(s) anybody ever had. And it's funny, but I feel as if I've known you all the time. But I couldn't have, could I?

I also have my three children to thank. In some ways, Jennifer, Karen and Dave led the way with their own honest questions about the faith in which they were raised as preacher's kids.

To the keen and careful editor Susan Greer, the creative graphic designer Amanda Boltë and the indispensable Richard Bain, publisher of Binea Press, thank you for your belief in this project. And to all who have anticipated my words from pulpit and in print every week for four decades, you have pulled the best out of me and helped me believe that the best is yet to come. Together we continue the miraculous 3.5-billion-year continuity of life on Earth from one generation to the next, glorious in its contiguity and breathtaking in its contemplation.

Finally, I thank the dedicatee of this book, my wife Deb, who married a minister but has loved the man. Tuus perdite sodalist amans.

Unless indicated, all scripture verses are from the New American Standard Bible.

· PREFACE ·

The truth is the one thing nobody will believe.
Bernard Shaw (The Man of Destiny)

I once led the largest mainline Protestant congregation in Canada. Over the years, its pulpit was occupied by some of the most gifted orators my country has produced, both liberal and evangelical in their approach to the proclamation of the Christian faith. For 15 years, I applied my oratorical skills to continue this congregation's grand tradition of a passionate and articulate telling of the good news of Christianity.

Today I am an atheist. This book is the testimony of my deconversion.

In courts of law, people are called to give testimony. They do not have to defend or denigrate the accused. That is the job of defence lawyers and Crown attorneys or prosecutors. The one giving testimony says who they are, where they were, what they saw and how they felt.

In Christian evangelical circles, people are also called to give testimony. They do not have to preach a sermon or argue for God's existence. They do not have to prove a blessed thing. That is the task assigned to those trained in systematic theology or homiletics. Those giving a testimony of faith, not unlike courtroom witnesses, are called to articulate their experiences; to tell their stories. I was at this place at this time and this is what happened to me. All that is demanded is the truth, the whole truth and nothing but the truth.

Christian testimony tends to be a tale of conversion. *I once was lost and now I'm found*, as John Newton put it in his hymn *Amazing Grace*. At a meeting in the upper room on Aldersgate Street in London, England on May 24, 1738, John Wesley heard part of Martin Luther's commentary on the Book of Romans and had his conversion experience. His famous testimony was a journal entry: "I felt my heart strangely warmed. I felt I did trust in Christ, Christ alone for salvation; and an assurance was given me that He had taken away my sins, even mine, and saved me from the law of sin and death."[1]

Testimony carries great import because, while the truth of someone's story may not be everyone's truth and may be scoffed at by others, the witness is unlikely to be swayed by dissent. There's a line in an old song recorded by the Doobie Brothers, co-written by Michael McDonald and Kenny Loggins.

What a fool believes he sees, no wise man has the power to reason away.[2]

And yet. What if someone feels compelled to give a testimony, not of conversion, but of deconversion; to suggest that while he once believed, reason had dispelled faith?

This is my journey, first to faith and then from faith. I do not for a moment assume my story carries an intrinsic power to dispel someone's beliefs. It is one more story to add to everyone's story. It is not everyone's truth but it is my truth. It is not everyone's journey, but it is my journey.

So I invite you to walk with me as I point to epiphanies or signposts in my sojourn and how they propelled me toward atheism. No one insight stands as a definitive argument why there is almost certainly no God. For instance, when I begin by talking about the unpleasant nature of the Abrahamic God, it is not an argument that a deity you don't like must not exist, but a realization that our deities too often reflect the darker sides of our nature and the God who is described in scripture often fails to resemble the God we sell ourselves in order to buttress our own beliefs.

To repeat, like someone whose journey to faith is circuitous, so also is my journey. I began to follow a path wherever it would lead me and with each insight and reflection, the foundations of my faith began to crumble. In the testimony of my deconversion you may come to understand, even if you cannot agree, how someone who once preached with passion and sincerity can now say, "I was wrong."

1 John Wesley, Percy Livingstone Parker, and Augustine Birrell, *The Heart of John Wesley's Journal* (New York,: Fleming H. Revell Co., 1903), 43.

2 *What A Fool Believes* lyrics © Kenny Loggins — Gnossos Music and Milk Money Music, Universal Music Publishing Group

CHAPTER ONE

· PILGRIMAGE TO THE PULPIT ·

Jesus loves me this I know, for the Bible tells me so;
Little ones to him belong. They are weak, but he is strong.

Anna Bartlett Warner

My pilgrimage to the pulpit began very early. By the time I was born in Chatham Ontario, I had already been attending an Anglican church for nine months. A few years later I was a cherubic choirboy bedecked in white surplice and frilly collar. I had perfect attendance at Sunday School. As a teenager I became a server (the Protestant equivalent of an altar boy) and began to teach Sunday School.

In my fervour and youthful exuberance, I wanted to update the church's music with my guitar and promote Jesus as the quintessential hippie. I put up a poster in the church depicting Jesus as a "Wanted" revolutionary[3]. It was promptly torn down. I was disheartened. I wrote a letter to the rector of the congregation informing him of my decision to resign from the posts I held in the congregation at the time. I walked out the door. A dear friend who lived across the street from our home knew my distress. He also knew a local United Church minister. We were introduced and soon, at age 19, I found my way up the street from a congregation in the Anglican Church of Canada to a congregation in the United Church of Canada. My parents were sad that I'd left the church of my birth, but they understood my frustrations and supported my decisions. Arriving at this new church with guitar in hand, I was welcomed with open arms, made fast friends, welcomed Jesus into my heart, began to speak and sing in public and soon became a candidate for ordained ministry.

I began to devour books that would feed and fuel my faith. Hal Lindsey's *The Late Great Planet Earth* suggested Jesus was about to return to Earth. I couldn't wait! Francis Schaeffer's *The God Who Is There* and Josh McDowell's *Evidence Which Demands a Verdict* confirmed what I already believed. Christianity was true and could stand up to any argument against it. I was a full-blown Jesus freak with bell-bottom jeans, macramé cross, long hair and beard.

I felt I had found my vocation, my calling. I felt that Christian ministry was what I was born to do. Some are called to be doctors or lawyers. I felt called to be a preacher and I quickly fell in love with what I was doing.

For the next six years, I played lead guitar in a Christian band. We hauled our equipment to any venue where people would listen to us, from traditional worship services, coffee houses and all-night gospel sings to park bandshells and summer camps. You name it. We criss-crossed the country and released one album.

At the same time, I earned the requisite university degrees and was ordained to serve the church as a minister for the next 30 years. For four of those years I worked for a Christian relief and development organization, travelling throughout the Third World to scout out development projects, returning to Canada eager to raise money to support everything from cottage industries and school lunch programs to community health initiatives.

Along the way, I hosted a weekly two-hour syndicated radio show of contemporary Christian music called *Night Light*. I also hosted a local cable television program showing Christian music videos. I was always active in ecumenical efforts to bridge the gaps between denominations. I helped to launch the Christian Churches Network of London (www.ccnl.org). For the last 15 years of my ecclesiastical career, I was the senior minister of Metropolitan United Church in London, Ontario. With over 2500 active members, it was the largest mainline Protestant congregation in Canada. I was one of a group of clergy who met annually with the prime minister of the day (Jean Chretien, Paul Martin, Steven Harper) to share our thoughts on domestic policy from Christian perspectives. You could not fault me for lack of sincerity and enthusiasm.

My vocation meant that I gave up weekends for most of my adult life. I could not attend out-of-town Saturday weddings of family and friends. I was always on call to comfort the bereaved. Friday nights brought rehearsals for weddings at which I would be officiating the next day. I rarely went out on Saturday night, opting to remain cloistered with the sermon for Sunday. I did not complain then and I do not complain now. I accepted the demands and restrictions that came with my vocation. The highlight of my week was when I stood to deliver the 25-minute monologue I had written and, for the most part, memorized.

For most of the year, my family paid a price for my calling. Too often I was unavailable or preoccupied by the demands of so many people who were a family of faith. There were times, I'm ashamed to admit, that Jennifer, Karen and David did not have a father to tuck them into bed at night. I wasn't home. I had meetings to chair and people to comfort. Family vacations were timed by the ebb and flow of the main events in the church year to minimize the impact of my absence. Mine was a "pulpit church", which meant the congregation expected their senior minister to preach practically every Sunday. I rarely let them down, continuing to preach without interruption through the traumatic seasons of life which include death and divorce.

Seven-day work weeks were not uncommon. I was busy but joyfully busy. Every year, right after the annual meeting of the congregation in February, I would get sick. I toiled gladly but feverishly through Christmas into the new year to get the congregation ready for its deliberations over money and plans. Once the meeting was over and pressure was off, my body was free to give in to illness. I looked at it all not as a price to pay but part of what it meant to serve Christ in a congregation of such demands and potential; a people who brought to Sunday services an expectation of excellence and anticipation of inspiration. I was convinced this was God's will for my life and I gladly chose to do it with as much creativity and energy as I could muster.

To keep my mind sharp after turning 50, I embarked on a doctoral program from a seminary in California. I completed my course work and began work on my thesis paper. The topic was to explore ways to preach objective universal truths in a postmodern world that doesn't recognize objective truth.

I offer this short synopsis, this list of my solid Christian credentials, partly to answer in advance the criticism some believers throw at former believers: that they never really believed in the first place. Let me assure you. I really believed. I was going to heaven and I desperately wanted everyone else to go to heaven too.

But in the fall of 2009 at age 57, to the surprise and, for the most part, disappointment of my congregation, I took early retirement. I had watched colleagues stay too long at the fair and swore that I would never be one of those clergy whose last years tended to undo the good of their earlier years because they didn't know when to quit. As they say, you should always leave the party before the hosts start flicking the lights off and on. But by that time, unbeknown to almost everyone, my pilgrimage to the pulpit had taken a radical turn. For many reasons, I was wrestling with classic cognitive dissonance, a preacher laden by the burden of incredulity. I was asking myself questions, which only led to more and more questions. Curiosity is an amazing accelerant.

I started to struggle with the hypocrisy of trying to convince others of a message of which I was increasingly unconvinced. I was starting to understand religion as a human construct or, to borrow from William Blake, a "mind-forg'd manacle."[4] I began to understand that like the long line of deities in the history of our species, the Abrahamic God made manifest in Jesus was not only a projection of our need for a First Cause, our tendency to avoid looking fate in the face or our desire for an edge over our enemies, but also a reflection of our violent, jealous, misogynistic, intolerant image.

To put it simply, my mind had changed. I had embarked on a new journey. This book, then, is the story of a pilgrimage from the pulpit and how my deconversion has transformed my life in ways which are no less radical and joyful than conversion.

Why "come out," as it were? Why not keep my doubts to myself?

I have misgivings about this book. For starters, autobiography is audaciously telling the world how you are before they have asked. How could I be so presumptuous as to assume anyone would care what I think at this point in my life?

Second, a part of me would like to keep this story as my secret, lest people think less of me and tell me so. But I also know how ugly and crippling secrets are and that it is important every once in awhile to tell the secret of who we are because otherwise, we can lose track of who we truly are. We risk coming to believe the edited version of ourselves, which we hope the world will find acceptable.

I rigorously questioned my motives for writing this book. Am I caught up in the reverse of the convert's zeal? Am I trying to disabuse believers? Do I have some axe to grind? If faith is merely personal benign belief, why upset someone else's spiritual apple cart? Why be less than sanguine towards religious conviction?

Here are three reasons for this book. For starters, belief is not benign. Private faith has a public face. From Torquemada to the Taliban, the zealotry and bigotry that flow from spiritual certainties have been platforms to launch savage clashes between countries and cultures. The unreflective credence afforded ancient texts has led to censorship, conformity, control and the closure of minds.

People with authority, real or imagined, have co-opted faith to secure their power and line their pockets by fleecing the gullible. In politics, religion is used to suppress science and shore up a conservative social agenda. The fight against condom distribution in AIDS-ravaged Africa or stem cell research in the USA come to mind.

Religious zealots who are pathologically fixated on death and the apocalypse are prepared to hasten both as a means to purify this world and usher in the next one. As neuroscientist Sam Harris points out, "Ten years have passed since a group of mostly educated and middle-class men decided to obliterate themselves, along with three thousand innocents, to gain entrance to an imaginary Paradise."[5] I'll have more to say about this in my chapter on The End.

Another motive for this book is rooted in the notion that all of us, religious or not, ought to value authenticity. If we do, then our discourse should encourage not only critical thinking but intellectual honesty without fear of rejection or reprisal. My disclosure carries the risks of losing friends and facing disappointment and disapproval from those who once admired my spirituality. However, personal integrity urges me, in the words of King Lear's Fool, to speak what I feel, not what I ought to say. As a result, the notions and questions in this book might sound harsh, my conclusions polemical, particularly to those whose faith is a source of great joy and consolation. "You can challenge my loyalties in hockey or politics but leave my religion alone!"

I understand the sensitivities but I cannot let them silence me. Religion tends to protect itself from scrutiny and challenge by demanding deference and respect. Like the movie manifestation of the great and powerful Wizard of Oz, ecclesial smoke and bluster are designed to impress and intimidate. When you peer behind the curtain of sacred mysteries, however, you find just an ordinary human being.

The overriding motive for this book, however, is pastoral. The heart that was once surrendered to Christ, that gave itself to others and that infused my vocation with kindness, still beats in me. What you read is not the angry rant of a disgruntled cleric. It is, rather, the honest account of one person's journey from faith to reason.

There's an old saw that preaching should comfort the afflicted and afflict the comfortable. I believe, and I hope, the story of my deconversion may comfort the afflicted. Most non-believers keep their silence, not articulating their decision to eschew the dogma of faith so as not to offend and not feel isolated. Today, those who are wrestling with the tenets of religion or the increasing insights of science may be comforted to know they are not alone. There is life beyond belief.

At the same time my story may afflict the comfortable; urging committed believers to take their spiritual convictions seriously, examine evidence they may never have encountered before and determine if they can still believe with integrity.

---

3   http://www.flickr.com/photos/whsimages/4196049832/

4   The phrase comes from Blake's poem *London*

5   http://www.samharris.org/blog/item/september-11-2011

CHAPTER TWO

· A DISTASTEFUL DEITY ·

Gods always behave like the people who created them.

Zora Neale Hurston

I think the first step in my sojourn was taken unknowingly during one of the responsive readings of the Psalms as I led Sunday morning worship in 2007. Over the years I had been through arid seasons in my faith, times when it felt like I was in the wilderness needing some spiritual sustenance to slake my thirst. Most people of faith go through those times. I once confided in a colleague that I was feeling spiritually dry. He recommended the works of New Testament scholar and retired Anglican bishop N.T. Wright. I read Wright's books voraciously to get me out of the desert so to speak. They helped. I had weathered the storms of divorce and the sudden accidental death of my mother as a result of an impaired driver still convinced of my beliefs. But this was different. Somehow, for reasons that I will never fully understand, and for the first time, I started to listen to what I was reading in the Bible.

God was jealous. I knew that already. God didn't like competition from other deities or objects of worship. The first of the Ten Commandments was that "you shall have no other gods before Me." Check. There may be other gods but Yahweh demanded exclusivity, though I never did quite understand why God would be jealous of other deities if he was the creator of everything that exists.

God was everywhere and could do anything and knew everything, from the answer to every question to all the thoughts in my head.

I always knew the relationship between God and humanity is modelled on the structure of an absolute monarchy: kings must be praised, feared, fawned over, obeyed, loved and followed. We are commanded to love this God and threatened with eternal anguish if we don't believe in our hearts that this God exists.

But I was starting to pick up on God's character traits, which are not only mutually contradictory but downright unsavoury. The psalmist in the reading on that particular Sunday was asking God to take sides in a war and kill the enemy. God is always on our side, of course. But as I continued to read the Bible in public and in private over subsequent weeks, God was starting to come across as not only vindictive against enemy tribes but petulant and petty, cruel and capricious, a deity with anger management issues coupled with an obsessive craving for praise. This deity sounded more like a malevolent bully than the God of peace and love formed in my imagination in infancy. He was as fickle and unreliable as humans.

Psalm 137, for instance, which begins with the familiar lament of a people in exile, "By the rivers of Babylon, there we sat down and wept when we remembered Zion"... ends with a blessing for anyone who retaliates against the Babylonians: "How blessed will be the one who seizes and dashes your little ones against the rock." (Psalm 137:9) Anyone today who would kill a child by smashing her into a rock would be considered a homicidal maniac to be hunted down, convicted of the crime and incarcerated for life. But here, God would bless him.

The prophet Hosea wrote, "Samaria ... has rebelled against her God; they will fall by the sword. Their little ones will be dashed in pieces, and their pregnant women will be ripped open" (Hosea 13:16). Let that one sink in for a moment.

In Numbers 15:32-36, the people of Israel find a man gathering sticks on the Sabbath. They arrest him and ask God what to do with him. God tells Moses they should stone him. Was this fellow gathering sticks to make a fire to cook supper for his wife and child or even to make a sacrifice? Who knows? All we know is that he broke the rule about working on the Sabbath and God sentenced him to death.

In my mind, this all-powerful One was coming across as thin-skinned and quick-tempered, especially when it came to the problem of blasphemy. In the movie *Life of Brian*, Monty Python's satirical take on first-century messiah mania, Brian Cohen accompanies his mother as she joins other women, disguised as men, in the stoning of a local blasphemer. This old man's defence to the charge of "uttering the name of our Lord" is, "Look, I'd had a lovely supper and all I said to my wife was 'That piece of halibut was good enough for Jehovah.' " Hilarious.

But if you read the Old Testament, blasphemy is no laughing matter. In Leviticus 24, the son of an Israelite woman and an Egyptian "blasphemed the Name, and cursed." We don't know what profanation this reprobate uttered. He may have suffered a momentary burst of enthusiasm as in the case of the Python blasphemer. Still, the man was brought before Moses and placed in custody waiting for God to pronounce sentence. God says to Moses, "Bring the one who has cursed outside the camp, and let all who heard him lay their hands on his head; and let all the congregation stone him. And say to the people of Israel, Whoever curses his God shall bear his sin. He who blasphemes the name of the Lord shall be put to death; all the congregation shall stone him; the foreigner as well as the native, when he blasphemes the Name, shall be put to death" (Leviticus 24:14-16).

I started to think of the morality of God; the behaviours we consider good and those not so good. In the Bible, God is portrayed as one who is obsessed with punishing sexual misconduct while at the same time engaging in infanticide. According to the book of Exodus, to entice Pharaoh to let the enslaved people of Israel go, God allegedly killed the first-born babies of the Egyptians. To do this, the Israelites marked the doorposts of their homes with blood so that the angel of death would pass over them in his task of infanticide. You have to wonder why a supernatural being could not tell the difference between houses of Jews and Egyptians unless there was blood on the door, but that's the kind of detail we tend to overlook.

At any rate, the God of love allegedly slaughtered babies whose only crime was to be born into the wrong side of a struggle at the wrong time in history.

Today, our justice system would incarcerate one who would murder a baby. Rather than being the kind shepherd of David, the God of Moses started to feel like an amoral tyrant. What if I had been an Egyptian father who believed Pharaoh should go ahead and free the people of Israel but despite my opinion, had my first-born child murdered by the Israelites' God in an attempt to persuade Pharaoh? How would I feel about that God?

I started to think about the justice of God. As the gospel goes, when you die, if you have accepted Jesus as your lord and saviour, you go to heaven. If you don't, you suffer in hell for eternity. So the deathbed confession of a scoundrel is rewarded with eternal bliss, but a wonderful person who does not accept Jesus into his or her heart is punished forever. Doesn't justice mean the punishment should fit the crime? For the crime of not believing God exists or believing in the "wrong" god for the few short years of our lifetime, a soul is sentenced to suffer unspeakable torment for eternity. It didn't seem very just. Something wasn't feeling right.

In light of these unlikeable traits, I started to think about the love for this God that forms the foundation of Christian faith. What was it about this God that we were to adore? His love, of course. His amazing grace. He loved us so much that he gave his son to die for us, according to John 3:16. But then I started to think about this old, old story. God needed a sacrifice to forgive our sins. (Why couldn't God just say "I forgive you", like humans are often called to do?) So God gave up his son to be born of a virgin, to live for about 30 years and then be tortured and executed in payment for our transgressions.

With great respect to the horrors of crucifixion and not attempting to make light of an execution, Jesus had a very bad weekend. But then what happened? He came to life again and, according to the ancient Nicene Creed, returned to his former glory with God the heavenly Father and that's where he reigns today!

If you accept the doctrine of the Trinity, one God manifest in three persons, God lost nothing. Thousands of parents have sacrificed their children to horrible deaths in human conflict to guarantee our freedom. Their children never came back. What about the firefighters who rushed into the World Trade Centre on 9/11 to try to save people they didn't even know? They forfeited their lives, died a ghastly death and didn't come back to life. So we are mandated to love God for giving up his son as a sacrifice. But if you go to the end of the gospel story, God never lost his son at all. The son still reigns today and allegedly is interceding for us in response to our supplications.

Are there any other reasons for us to love God? Well, frankly, we are commanded to do it in submission to God's authority. "Our God is an awesome God, He reigns from heaven to earth." intones the praise chorus. What kind of love is contingent on authority, punishment or reward?

Is real love not rooted in admiration and respect freely given without the assurance of reward or threat of punishment? This distasteful characteristic is not offered as a proof that God does not exist. But if He does exist and if He is anything like the biblical characterization, I'm not enamoured with such a deity and hardly prone to offer worship and praise.

I have long been uncomfortable with the place of women in organized religion. Scripture has been carefully quoted to justify giving women a role unequal to that of men. Those who put women in their place in church are the men who are holding on to their place in the church and men, sadly, still tend to make the rules. Not surprisingly, a deity created by patriarchal goat herders is going to be patriarchal.

Why was this dark side of the character of God appearing to me at age 55 rather than age 35? Life was good. I was happily married and my ministry at Metropolitan was in fine form. I simply started to look at my faith in a different light.

Believers may be shocked to hear of the genocide and infanticide encouraged by the God described in the Bible. They may be unable to hear the Christian message as heard for the first time by, say, an alien from outer space, that a long time ago, God made an entire universe in order to have a relationship with one species of primate on one of the planets in one of the billions of galaxies, us. The first woman, made from a man's rib was convinced by a talking snake to eat the fruit of a certain tree. In doing that, she disobeyed this God who was so angry he demanded the death penalty. He could not forgive disobedience unless blood was shed from a perfect sacrifice. Centuries of ritual animal slaughtering wasn't cutting it and since no human is perfect, God provided the perfect sacrifice by impregnating a young virgin with himself as her child so he could have himself be killed as the perfect sacrifice to himself. That way, those who offer thanks for the sacrifice of this perfect man (who was his own father), and who telepathically tell him they accept him as the master of their life, will live forever.

Believers will, of course, counter with the need to interpret biblical details metaphorically, symbolically or mystically, particularly in the context of a plan of salvation that is allegedly unfolding.

This of course raises a new set of questions. Which parts are to be taken literally and which parts are to be taken figuratively? And how do you know which interpretation to take for which part? Once I started to feel offended by God's very personality, the next step was to get back into my Bible. It, after all, is the proverbial Good Book. As I revisited the alleged word of God, I read passages as if for the first time. They were further signposts along the road.

CHAPTER THREE
· THE NOT-SO-GOOD BOOK ·

*The Old Testament is responsible for more atheism, agnosticism,
disbelief — call it what you will — than any book ever written.*
A.A. Milne (creator of Winnie the Pooh)

The things that you're li'ble to read in the Bible, it ain't necessarily so.
Ira Gershwin (Porgy and Bess)

To believe in the Bible it helps not to read it.
@TheTweetOfGod

I still have my first Bible, a zippered, illustrated, leather, King James Version with my name stamped on the cover. *Robert C. Ripley.* My grandmother inscribed it to let me know it was a gift for Christmas Day, 1962. I loved the feel of this book. I loved looking at the pictures when I was growing up. Simple titles for each portrait. *Noah's Ark. David and Goliath. Moses and the Tablets. Jesus Healing the Sick.*

Like most Christians, I always believed the Bible is a good book, perhaps the most profound book ever, an all-time bestseller because its themes of goodness and love have stood the test of time.

The Bible has given us expressions we use all the time without knowing their source: the skin of your teeth; the root of the matter; a fly in the ointment; a drop in the bucket; wolves in sheep's clothing; it is better to give than receive; to fall from grace; to suffer fools gladly. All are phrases from the beloved King James Version of the Bible.

Sure, there were stories that defy credulity–Jonah and the whale and all that. But what was becoming clear to me was that those who elevate holy writ as inspired by God, either literally or metaphorically, those who consider it a source book for morality and good living, are forced to approach the Bible like a smorgasbord, picking out the plausible or pleasant parts and disregarding the rest.

I realized this because I began to take the Bible more seriously than ever before. I studied it more carefully than ever before. Did I believe a talking snake was the smartest of all the animals (Genesis 3:1) and that God cursed it for tempting Eve by putting it on its belly? Wasn't it already on its belly? Did I believe that Eve was created from Adam's rib, according to the second of two different creation stories in the book of Genesis? If I didn't believe the Genesis creation stories and considered them metaphoric, then what parts of the Bible did I believe actually happened? Did all the animals on the planet live within walking distance of Noah's Ark?

We've heard about Moses coming down from the mountain carrying stone tablets on which God had written the Ten Commandments. Unfortunately for the commandments, Moses smashed the tablets in a fit of anger because the Israelites had chosen to worship a golden calf in Moses' absence. (Exodus 32:19) This was God's first direct work as an author and now it was lost! No problem. God, being God, was capable of salvaging the matter. God told Moses he'd write on a new set of tablets "the words that were on the first" (Exodus 34:1). The second Ten Commandments are close to the first, but not duplicates by any means. Later on we find yet another version of the Ten Commandments (Deuteronomy 5).

You might think something as important as 10 mandates from God would not have three different versions. While some of the differences are merely their order, there are clear distinctions. For instance, the version in Exodus 20:11 requires keeping the Sabbath because "in six days the Lord made the heavens and the earth, the sea, and all that in them is, and rested on the seventh day." But in Deuteronomy 5:15, Jews are told to "remember that you were a slave in the land of Egypt, and the Lord your God brought you out of there by a mighty hand and by an outstretched arm; therefore the Lord your God commanded you to observe the sabbath day." Nothing is said about God resting after the six days it took to create the universe.

I found myself poring over biblical passages which, to my shame and chagrin, I'd never come across in all my years of ministry. I was dismayed to discover huge portions of the Bible that, for obvious reasons, never made it into Vacation Bible School curricula or were chosen to be part of the Lectionary, a systematic collection of scripture readings appointed for Christian or Judaic worship over a three-year cycle. Here are a few examples.

Almost everyone has heard of Noah and the ark and how God was not happy with humans and so, in righteous anger, he drowned them all (including children and animals) except for one fortunate family.

Quite apart from the ruthlessness of killing everybody because you're not pleased with some or all of them, if you continue reading you discover what happened after the floodwaters subsided. Noah planted the first vineyard, sampled too much fruit of his vine and would take to lying naked in his tent. His sons would have to back into the tent to keep from seeing dad naked and cover up the poor man with a blanket (Genesis 9:23).

Then there's the story of Sodom and Gomorrah, the twin cities of sin that God fried. Abraham's nephew Lot was spared because he was considered a righteous man. When they were fleeing the firestorm, Lot's wife made the mistake of looking back when she'd been told not to and was turned into a pillar of salt. Isn't that a rather severe sentence for a relatively mild offence of peeking over your shoulder? Oh well, God sets the rules and metes out the punishments.

But what about the rest of the story, before and after the judicial bonfire of brimstone? Two male angels were sent to Lot's house to warn him to get out of town. Lot welcomed the angels but the men of the city started pounding on the front door demanding that Lot hand them over so that they could sodomize them. Lot refused. What a gallant guy! Then he said, "Why don't you take my virgin daughters and have your way with them instead?" It is difficult to imagine any father, let alone a man considered to be righteous, giving up his daughters to be raped in place of two angels. What a dastardly dad!

After the obliteration of Sodom, Lot and his traumatized daughters made their home in a cave in the mountains. Starved for men, the girls decided to get their father drunk and rape him. As the story of this horribly dysfunctional family ends, Lot's daughters are impregnated by their father (Genesis 19:36).

We've heard how Joshua shouted and the trumpets blew and the walls of Jericho came a' tumbling down. The rest of the story is in the next verse where good ol' Joshua did some ethnic cleansing and made sure that they "utterly destroyed all that was in the city, both man and woman, young and old, and ox, and sheep, and ass, with the edge of the sword." (Joshua 6:21) The city of Jericho was then burned. The silver, gold and articles of bronze and iron were spared and put into the treasury of the house of the Lord (Joshua 6:24) in return, I suppose, for God's generosity and complicity in what you might call the first genocide or extermination of a people.

Jephthah was one of Israel's judges who made a vow to God in exchange for a victory against the Ammonites. He would sacrifice, as a burnt offering, the first person who came out of the house to greet him on his return.

Jephthah slaughtered the Ammonites. Hurray. But who should greet him at home with tambourines and dancing but his daughter, his only child. Who did he expect? Jephthah kept his vow to God but unlike the case of Abraham, who was stopped at the last second and didn't have to sacrifice his son Isaac, God didn't intervene this time and Jephthah cooked his daughter (Judges 11).

What do we do with the grisly parts of these and other stories of scripture? Some accept them as true. According to pollster Gallup, about 50 per cent of the United States electorate still take Christian scriptures literally. But what does it mean to take scripture literally? Do you condone such barbarism?

Almost all the civilized world today agrees slavery is an abomination. No person should own another person. Period. Today, when we hear of young girls caught and sold as slaves, we also hear of kind, courageous people who venture into harm's way to buy them back and set them free.

What does the Bible have to say about slavery? There are clear, unambiguous taboos such as avoiding shellfish (Lev. 11:10), mixed fabrics (Deuteronomy 22:11), cross-dressing (Deuteronomy 22:5), round haircuts (Leviticus 19:27) and tattoos (Leviticus 19:28). Simple. Straightforward.

But God seems to have no problem with slavery (Leviticus 25:44-46). Once the Hebrew slaves were free, what edict would serve as a moral code to guide these former slaves? Israelites must treat each other with kindness and respect, and it is forbidden for them to own each other (Lev. 25:42). They know the horror of slavery first hand. If a Hebrew is sold to a Hebrew, they are to be treated kindly as an indentured servant and set free after six years loaded up with food, wine and livestock (Deuteronomy 15:12-15). Slaves for the Israelites are to come from the nations around them (Leviticus 25:44), as well as the people whose cities they want to invade (Deuteronomy 20:10-11). They can then bequeath them to their sons so that they are in bondage permanently (Lev. 25:46). Unless it is a runaway slave seeking asylum (Deuteronomy 23:15), a deal is a deal.

There are a few provisions, mind you. If you beat a slave who dies, you should be punished but if he lives a day or two, "no vengeance shall be taken; for he is his property." (Exodus 21:21) If you strike the eye of a slave you have to set him free. Likewise if you knock out his teeth. Men are even free to sell their daughters as sex slaves (Exodus 21:7-11). Jesus said nothing about slavery. St. Paul, however, does admonish slaves to serve their masters well.

If you're in search of moral guidance, some will point to the hallowed Ten Commandments. In 2003 I preached a 10-part series over 10 weeks called Smoke on the Mountain (a nod to the band *Deep Purple*, of course). A sermon for every commandment from Yahweh. They are the only writings of scripture that the creator of the universe felt were so important, they needed to be inscribed in his own handwriting in stone.

The first four commandments have nothing to do with what we normally consider moral codes applicable to all people. They forbid any beliefs outside the Judeo/Christian tradition, saying the wrong words or working on the Sabbath.

Some commandments do offer common moral standards. Don't kill or lie or cheat and so on. As laudable as those injunctions are, similar prohibitions have been part of our species long before Moses made it down from the mountain. Besides, Christians have oppressed, enslaved, tortured and killed others in God's name for centuries. It is true that just because people don't follow God's law, it is not a reflection on the God who gives the law. But there is nothing in the Ten Commandments that is helpful to the workings of civilized society that cannot be found elsewhere.

Christian apologists will argue that not everything recorded in the Bible happened. How could Noah herd every species of life on Earth into a boat somewhere in Turkey? How could Joshua's shout raze walls? Fair enough.

But if only parts of the Bible are historically true, who decides what did or did not happen? Choosing between history and allegory is highly subjective. If some events didn't happen, how do we elevate the entire Old and New Testaments as the *"inspired, the only infallible, authoritative Word of God,6"* as is the stance of some? It became clear to me that those who maintain the Bible is an inerrant source of righteous rules for living have not read the whole story. Are we to emulate its maniacal nationalism and vindictive laws?

So many preachers elevate the Bible as a guide for family values, a solid foundation on which to build a marriage. I readily and sadly count myself among them. But do we really want to follow the Bible's guidelines for matrimony? As for finding a wife, scripture has some methods which are at best unconventional and at worse immoral. Moses found a man with seven daughters and impressed the father by helping to water his flock. For these efforts, Moses was given one of the daughters, Zipporah.

David cut the foreskins off 200 of King Saul's Philistine enemies. For his gallant, albeit unorthodox efforts, David was given Michal's hand in marriage. Later on, David fell in love with the infamous Bathsheba. The only obstacle was her husband. David solved that little problem by ensuring Uriah was killed in battle. God was not happy about this dastardly road to the altar and neither were David's sons.

As punishment, God allegedly said to David, "I will raise up evil against you from your own household; I will take your wives before your eyes, and give them to your companion, and he shall lie with your wives in broad daylight" (2 Samuel 12:11). When Uriah's widow bore a child to David, God struck the child with sickness. Seven days later the child died (2 Samuel 12:18). God killed an innocent child to punish the immorality of the child's father.

In the famous book of Job, God let Satan kill all of Job's children, betting on Job's fidelity.

In the book of Judges, a group of men hid in the vineyard at a party and when the women came out to dance, they each grabbed one and carried her off to be a wife. The book of Deuteronomy suggests that if you take a liking to a prisoner of war, bring her home, shave her head, trim her nails, buy her new clothes and she's yours. Period. (Deuteronomy 21:10-13)

If your brother died with no children, it was your duty to impregnate his wife, your sister-in-law. It was not only a strategy, it was the law. In Numbers 31, Moses tells his soldiers to "keep alive for yourselves" any virgins captured in war. Solomon increased the odds of finding Ms. Right with multiple wives. Modern family values?

Then there are the rules of the Old Testament that are as strange as they are comedic. Men with wounded penises or no testicles were not allowed in the synagogue (Deuteronomy 23:1).

God comes up with vile penalties for disobedience. In Leviticus 26:27-29 God warns the people that if they are hostile to God, God will be hostile to them and force them to eat their own babies.

The Bible says homosexuality is an abomination (Leviticus 18:22) but so also is eating shellfish, according to Leviticus 11:10. It says in Leviticus 25:44 that I may possess slaves, both male and female, provided they are from neighbouring nations. I know that I am allowed no contact with a woman while she is in her period of menstrual uncleanliness (Leviticus 15:19-24). If you have a neighbour who insists on working on the Sabbath, Exodus 35:2 clearly states he should be put to death. The neighbour violates Leviticus 19:19 by planting two different crops in the same field, as does his wife by wearing garments made of two different kinds of thread (cotton and polyester?). I kept asking myself what would motivate a deity to create such absurd guidelines and vengeful retributions?

We all know the story of the exodus of the people of Israel from slavery in Egypt to the promised land. After 40 years of wandering in the wilderness under Moses, the Israelites conquered the land called Canaan. How did they manage this? By remarkably bloody means, replete with massacres and the enslavement of women and children. God repeatedly directs the Israelites to commit ethnic cleansing (Exodus 34:11-14, Leviticus 26:7-9) and genocide against numerous cities and tribes: the Cananites, Hittites, Hivites, Perizzites, Girgashites, Amorites and Jebusites (Joshua 1-12). How is this justified? Because the Israelites are the chosen people (Deuteronomy 7:6), singled out by God and exalted above all others.

What are our options with these gruesome texts? Those who have actually read the Bible will not be surprised at the depraved moral implications of these Old

Testament passages and my reaction to them. Some who espouse the inviolate truth of the Bible have elected to bite the bullet and assume that if God was the author of these morally embarrassing edits and episodes, there was something in the context that made them somehow morally right at the time.

Another response is that God doesn't have to play by the same rules as we do. In other words, if God wants to act a certain way or establish a certain rule, then it's "moral" because God does it. It may be unjust that God plays by a different set of rules than we are asked to observe but God made us and rules over us and, well, that's just the way it is.

At this point in my journey, I was becoming convinced that rather than being the best book ever written, whose subject was a God I should adore, the Bible reveals a deity who, by any modern standard of human morality, was depraved. How could I possibly promote a God of love who kills defenseless babies?

As I look back, my mind was undergoing a fundamental transformation. After re-reading the Bible and delving into sections I had previously ignored or glossed over, I went from adoring God to disliking God immensely. As I said earlier, just because you don't like a deity doesn't mean the deity does not exist. There are a lot of people whose personality and behaviour I dislike, and they definitely exist. But it was God's depravity that led me to the realization that this God of the Bible was a creation and projection of people who, by nature, are prone to depravity, to being amoral and vengeful. In my mind, God as an objective reality did not, does not, exist.

I know the retort from Christians–that they are not bound to the Priestly Code of the Old Testament. I also hear the accusation that it is somehow deceitful to cherry-pick the ugly or strange stories and verses of the Bible. But those who believe the Bible tend to do exactly the same thing. They select from the whole book the parts that are palatable and pass over the unpleasant bits. They cite the good moral teachings against murder, stealing and lying. They pick out lovely verses from, say, Psalm 23 or the Sermon on the Mount or St. Paul's chapter on love (1 Corinthians 13) that graces most Christian wedding ceremonies, as representative of the whole of scripture. Sadly, they are not.

Many just ignore the Old Testament and point to Jesus as an exemplar of a new morality. Jesus taught the very admirable Golden Rule[7] about not doing something to someone you wouldn't want them to do to you. He talked about turning the other cheek and loving your neighbour who, as the parable of the Good Samaritan suggests, is anyone who needs you; definitely an ethic of peace and love and kindness toward others. Then read elsewhere in the New Testament from a letter allegedly written by St. Paul:

"For after all it is only just for God to repay with affliction those who afflict you, and to give relief to you who are afflicted and to us as well when the Lord Jesus shall be revealed from heaven with His mighty angels in flaming fire, dealing out retribution to those who do not know God and to those who do not obey the gospel of our Lord Jesus. And these will pay the penalty of eternal destruction away from the presence of the Lord and from the glory of His power..." (2 Thessalonians 1:6-9)

In short, holding up the entire Bible, cover to cover, as an exemplar of good behaviour was becoming impossible for me. I came to the opinion that, in many ways, modern morality, in which we abhor genocide, ban slavery, honour women and frown on burning daughters, is far superior to a morality that would have us execute disobedient children and celebrate cruel carnage with xenophobic relish.

I then began to question whether it is a good thing at all to have our morality come from a sacred word allegedly revealed to us by a higher authority. What is morality anyway? If we think of it as a system of reciprocal claims in which everyone is accountable to everyone else, do we even need a higher external authority? Further, if our morality comes from a divine authority, then believers need only look to their particular idea or interpretation of God, say, to decide what they are justified in doing. That way, it is easy to ignore the plight of those injured by our actions. You must die because God has mandated it as your punishment! Deferring to God instead of to those affected by our actions avoids accountability to others. What kind of morality is that?

As for the Bible's historical accuracy, liberal preachers and theologians maintain we shouldn't take the Bible to be a history text; that many events described in the Bible didn't happen. Noah didn't float an ark. The walls of Jericho didn't crumble. So why could I no longer accept the liberal line that the Bible, while not historically true, is true metaphorically, that it teaches wonderful lessons, that it is an inspiration to moral rectitude?

I thought of so many non-biblical stories I have read whose lessons can move me to tears and motivate me to be a better person, far more than the edicts and examples from the Bible.

I agree that if you look for them, you can find laudable lessons in the Bible about loving our neighbours and the rewards of being meek. But there are also wonderful lessons in *The Wizard of Oz* and *The Little Engine that Could*, lessons about the power of a positive attitude, say, or the notion that courage belongs to those who act bravely.

At the same time I was questioning the Bible's historicity and morality, I started to wrestle with the content of the New Testament. After all, it contained the good news I had been passionately proclaiming for so many years. By this point, I was no more confident that there was a Jesus who was the pre-existent Son of the living God than that there was a wizard from Kansas who accidentally landed his hot air balloon in the land of Oz. I began by revisiting the biblical scholarship I first encountered in college while training for ministry, but had either rejected or glossed over in my enthusiasm to complete my studies, graduate and get out into the trenches of parish warfare. This part of the journey led me to the main character of the New Testament, Jesus of Nazareth.

---

6   This view of Scripture is common to most evangelical Christians. The wording here is from the Statement of Faith of the Billy Graham Evangelistic Association http://billygraham.org/about/what-we-believe/

7   What we now call the "Golden Rule" or the concept of the ethic of reciprocity did not originate with Jesus. It has roots in a wide range of cultures and is a standard used by different civilizations to resolve conflicts. Many prominent religious figures and philosophers have restated its reciprocal nature in various forms.

CHAPTER FOUR

· THE LEGEND OF JESUS ·

There are many things that are true which it is not useful for the vulgar crowd to know; and certain things which although they are false it is expedient for the people to believe otherwise.

St. Augustine, *City of God*

My lifelong image of Jesus remained relatively unchanged from my first introduction to him on the Sunday School felt-back cutout that stuck to the board covered in flannel and resting on an easel. It morphed into the counter-revolutionary hippie Christ of my late teens and finally matured in the miracle-working, universe-making, soon-returning-in-glory Messiah proclaimed in my adult ministry.

Now with a critical examination of the character of the God of the Old Testament and a fresh but disquieting read of the old, old Bible stories came questions about Jesus himself. Who was he, really? What did he say? What did he do? Did he exist at all or was he the figment of fertile first-century imaginations?

It is a painful stretch for a Christian to even consider the idea that Jesus either didn't exist or, if he did, that he isn't anyone beyond an obscure first-century teacher/prophet and bears little resemblance to the One worshipped on Sundays. After all, isn't Jesus enthroned at the very heart of Christianity, the object of adoration and the recipient of prayerful requests?

My quest for the historical Christ was, in fact, nothing new. Biblical scholars have been searching for him for decades. If there was a carpenter's son who came from Nazareth, how does he compare to the eternal Word of God incarnate who is proclaimed in the Bible and worshipped weekly?

Here's a quick overview of the search. An 18th century German scholar, Hermann Samuel Reimarus, suggested a separation between the Jesus of history and the Christ of faith. He argued that the real Jesus of Nazareth was a political revolutionary who died for his cause. Followers of this Jesus devised his resurrection, and a new religion, to try to make sense of what had happened. Reimarus' idea was downright dangerous at the time. His analysis of the historical Jesus was published posthumously.

Fast forward a century. In his book *Life of Jesus Critically Examined* (1835), David Strauss pointed out that we cannot read the gospels as historical biographies. They were written with one goal in mind: to win converts by attempting to convince the Jews that the messiah they had anticipated for centuries had arrived in Jesus of Nazareth. England's Earl of Shaftesbury attacked Strauss's book as the most pestilential book ever vomited out of the jaws of hell, the kind of review that would boost the sale of any tome.

But the inquiry into the question of who Jesus was gained respectability in 1904 with the publication of *The Quest for the Historical Jesus*. It was the work of a young New Testament scholar named Albert Schweitzer. Commonly known as a concert organist, physician, humanitarian and Nobel Peace Prize winner, Schweitzer wrestled, as others had before him, with the New Testament record. He concluded Jesus was a Jewish preacher who anticipated that God would intervene in history to overthrow the powers of evil. God would judge the world and set up a new kingdom of peace and justice on Earth, a Kingdom of God, within Jesus' own generation. While Schweitzer believed there was indeed a Jesus of Nazareth, he felt that Jesus bears no resemblance to the Christ of the stained-glass window.

I used to side with those who felt scholarly study of the scriptures is borderline blasphemy, since believers are to accept the Bible without question. God said it. I believe it. That settles it. But I also knew that if we are going to make the bold statement of faith that the Bible is the inerrant Word of God, that claim should be able to stand up to scholarly scrutiny.

So what did I now believe about Jesus? I returned to topics of New Testament study such as authorship, source material, internal and historical inconsistencies, as well as the context of first-century Palestine, to decide for myself who Jesus was if, in fact, he existed at all.

To shine some light on this portion of my path, I need to review the evidence we have for the New Testament. You can easily study it further on your own, and I would encourage you to do so. This review is simply to let you know what informed my conclusion.

First of all is the question of authorship. What records do we have, who wrote the books of the New Testament, and when were they written? We don't have the original gospels. They are long gone. Bear in mind that in those days if, say, Mark sat down and wrote a gospel and someone wanted a copy of it, they had to find someone to write out the copy. About 90 per cent of the population was illiterate. They couldn't read or write. Very few could do the work of making a copy. If, then, someone else wanted their gospel of Mark, they had to make a copy of the copy. What we have, then, are fragments of copies, of copies of copies made over the next thousand years.

If you've written or even typed a copy of a document written by hand, you know that without a spell-checker and proofreader, there are bound to be mistakes in spelling not to mention punctuation and grammar. Deciphering handwriting is usually the first challenge.

Now if someone takes your document and uses it to write out another version, your mistakes will be reproduced, along with their own mistakes. Sometimes the mistakes made by scribes were unintentional and insignificant. Sometimes the changes were intentional and significant. With each copy the variations compounded. At present we have about 5,000 copies of parts of the New Testament just in the Greek language alone.

Who wrote the gospels? Most scholars agree they were not likely written by the persons (Matthew, Mark, Luke and John) named in their titles. None of the writers identify themselves by name. The gospels come to us anonymously. We simply don't know who wrote them. Jesus' followers were lower-class Aramaic-speaking peasants from rural Galilee. They were almost certainly illiterate. The Bible says Peter and John were uneducated (Acts 4:13). How then could they write gospels in highly proficient Greek?

By the time the names of the reputed authors of the gospels were attached, other gospels surfaced that were read and revered by various groups of Christians. There were gospels alleged to have been written by Peter, Philip, Mary Magdalene and by Jesus' own brother Didymus Judas Thomas.

Even if you accept the tradition of authorship, Mark and Luke were not eyewitnesses to Jesus. Mark was allegedly the companion of Peter, who heard him preach about Jesus and compiled his teachings into a narrative. So if Mark was the author of the gospel, his information was second-hand.

Luke was said to be a physician who was a companion of St. Paul, who was not one of Jesus' disciples. We might assume Luke researched the life of Jesus and wrote his account. If that were the case, we would be dealing with an author who was a disciple of someone who was not a direct disciple of Jesus.

The truth, however, is that the gospels emerged decades after the date of Jesus' crucifixion (65-95 CE[8]) written by educated, Greek-speaking Christians who lived outside Palestine. So where did they get their material?

Most scholars place Mark as the earliest gospel, written around 70 CE. Matthew and Luke wrote 10 to 15 years later and seem to have had access to Mark's gospel and used it for some of their stories of Jesus, often verbatim. They also have independent traditions of Jesus' life and teachings in a source of the sayings of Jesus that scholars have called "sayings Quelle," or the "sayings source." Quelle is shortened to Q.

Luke's gospel contains material not found in Mark or Matthew,which suggests another source. Matthew as well has a special source of material about Jesus. John, the last of the four canonical gospels, is described as the "maverick gospel" because it is so different from the other three. So basically, the four gospels were a compilation of one other, combined with other long-lost written sources. And where did all this material come from in the first place, since the gospels were written decades after Jesus died?

The source is what we call oral tradition, which would include messages or stories transmitted verbally or in song—folktales and ballads, for instance.

There is one huge snag in this form of passing along information. When I was a kid we used to play a game called Buzz. We'd sit in a circle outside in the playground at recess. One person would whisper a sentence to the person next to them, who would whisper it to the next person and so on. After going full circle, the last person would say the sentence out loud and the person who started the sentence would tell us what they originally said. Usually, you'd hardly recognize the two sentences. The alterations were so wide-ranging they were laughable.

Word of mouth is and always will be highly malleable. Even when written down, stories and sayings constantly evolve. English poet Robert Southy wrote *The Story of the Three Bears* in 1837. He said his uncle had told him the story as a child. It was about an old woman who invades the house of three bears and then jumps out the window when they return home. As we know the story, the old woman has become a little girl named Goldilocks.

Just as tales evolve, hearsay and unreliable narrators have always been with us. Even today, with the benefit of ubiquitous cameras and the commentary of anyone with an Internet connection, pundits spin and exaggerate and misinterpret. As a result, we have developed a healthy skepticism about news stories and the blather of the blogosphere.

The Bible acknowledges this period of oral tradition. Luke begins his gospel indicating that he is using accounts that ministers of the Word have handed down (Luke 1:2). Paul also admits he is mentioning traditions inherited from believers before him: "For I delivered to you as of first importance what I also received, that Christ died for our sins..." (1 Corinthians 15:3).

Now imagine someone said something about the time U.S. President Kennedy was assassinated in 1963. No one wrote down what was said but the sayings and stories of this person were passed around until it occurred to people at the turn of the 21st century to write down, in a different language from the original, what had allegedly happened and been said. Over the next decade, people kept adding bits and pieces of information they had heard about what had been said or what had happened.

That's what we have in the decades of oral tradition between the death of Jesus and the unfolding record about him as the stories were altered in the telling and retelling. When you think of it this way, the discrepancies between the biblical books, the inconsistencies within the books and the plain improbabilities start to make sense.

The earliest fragment of a papyrus copy of John's gospel dates to about 130 CE. The first substantial physical evidence for the four Gospels comes from near the end of the second century or about 170 years after Jesus' death.

The earliest evidence of Christian communities doesn't come from gospels but from letters. St. Paul is our best example. Paul travelled the area around the Mediterranean Sea about 20 years after Jesus' death with a simple message that "Christ died for our sins according to the scriptures ... and that he was raised according to the scriptures." (1 Corinthians 15:3-4) No virgin birth. No resurrection appearances. No quotes from Jesus.

As Christians thirsted for details of this man who was proclaimed as the promised Messiah, gospels were written; lots of gospels, written pseudonymously. The gospel of Thomas is a collection of 114 sayings of Jesus from the early second century. The gospel of Peter is a fragmentary account of Jesus' trial, death and resurrection. There are about 40 other gospels down to the early Middle Ages, none of which are in the New Testament. They are filled with legend including tales of Jesus as a young boy using his miraculous power mischievously.

There were also stories about Jesus' followers. The Acts of the Apostles made it into the New Testament but there were the Acts of Paul, the Acts of Peter and the Acts of Thomas that didn't make the cut. In the first three centuries of Christianity, legends emerged about the followers of Jesus. Peter was known as one who could do spectacular miracles leading to massive conversions to the faith. As biblical scholar Bart Erhman has pointed out, Peter was said to have the power to heal the sick, cast out demons and raise the dead. Erhman writes, "Some of the stories about him will strike modern readers as more than a bit bizarre—as when he raises a smoked tuna fish from the dead in order to convince his onlookers of the power of God or when he deprives a maleficent magician of his power of flight over the city of Rome, leading to the magician's crash landing and death."[9]

The Bible includes epistles or letters written by Christian leaders to other Christians. Thirteen are attributed to St. Paul. There were other letters that claim to be written by Paul, as well as letters written in the names of other apostles which were not included in the Bible.

The early Christians were convinced Jesus was about to return from heaven and so they created prophetic accounts of what was going to happen. The New Testament ends with an apocalypse or revelation of the end of the world, Revelation, written by someone named John. But there were other apocalypses in circulation. One was allegedly written by Simon Peter. Another one, which was popular in the second century, was The Shepherd of Hermas.

When and how was the collection of letters and revelations and narratives shortened to the canon of scripture? Since the books of the New Testament didn't just appear on the scene shortly after Jesus' death, the business of deciding what writings were authoritative and what Christians therefore believed was raucous and rancorous. It wasn't until hundreds of years later that the familiar 27 books of the New Testament were listed together into one canon and consider authoritative.

What was becoming clear to me was that while there quite likely was a Jesus of Nazareth, the stories about him and the claims made about him evolved over decades. This just confirmed for me the notion that religion in general, and the story of Jesus in particular, is the result of human aspirations.

When all these scribes were copying and recopying the gospels, some alterations were likely inadvertent, while others were made to have the text say what the scribe thought it should say. Here are some random examples. When we meet Jesus in Mark's gospel, the oldest of the four gospels, Jesus is a grown man being baptized by John in the Jordan River. A word of divine favour echoes from heaven. In Mark, the voice says, "You are my Son, whom I love; with you I am well pleased," (Mark 1:11) as if to inform Jesus of something he doesn't know. In one Greek manuscript and several Latin versions of Luke, the voice quotes Psalm 2:7: "You are my Son, today I have begotten you", as if to suggest Jesus became the Son of God at his baptism. Only in Matthew does the voice out of heaven announce Jesus' divinity to the world. "This is My beloved Son, in whom I am well pleased" (Matthew 3:17).

In Mark, the pivotal events in the Christian narrative of the virgin birth and the resurrection do not appear at all. The story ends with an enigmatic empty tomb. Most Bibles note in the margin that the last 12 verses of Mark were added much later.

While I always preached on Easter Sunday that the glorious resurrection of Jesus was the main event of Christianity, I knew that Christmas was cultural Christianity's main event. Like so many, I love Christmas. Always have. I love the lights and the music, not to mention the mincemeat pie. When I was in ministry, I looked forward to planning a four-part series of sermons during the season of Advent, which anticipates Christmas. I loved all the extra services, particularly the late-night worship on Christmas Eve. Carols were sung with such gusto. I would proclaim Christ's glorious coming in the manger. At the end of the service, a holy family chosen from the congregation decked out as Mary, Joseph and their tiny baby would walk up the aisle to the front of the church while we all sang *Silent Night* in a darkened sanctuary. The image still gives me goosebumps.

But then on my journey, I ran into problems with the New Testament story of the baby born in a manger in Bethlehem.

Only two of the four canonical gospels, that is, the gospels of the New Testament, mention the birth of Jesus. The Christmas story we have come to know and love is a mixture of colour from the palettes of Matthew and Luke to paint a harmonious tableau, even though there are differences and discrepancies between the two accounts. In Luke's nativity story, Jesus' parents lived in Nazareth in the north of Galilee. A Roman census forces the family back to its ancestral city of Bethlehem in the south of Galilee near Jerusalem. While they are there, Jesus is born. The story is an invention because there was no empire-wide census and it seems highly unlikely that a Roman official would order people to be counted in cities their ancestors left years before. It would be like me travelling to Yorkshire, England today to be counted as part of the Ripley clan. Besides that, no census could have happened when "Quirinius was the governor of Syria," as Luke suggests, if Jesus was born when Herod was king. Quirinius did not become governor until 10 years after Herod's death.

So why did the author of Luke want to have Jesus of Nazareth born in David's City? Simple; to fulfil the Old Testament prophecy of Micah that the saviour would come from Bethlehem (Micah 5:2).

Matthew and Luke both include genealogies of Jesus. There are three problems here. The first is that both writers insist Jesus' mother was a virgin when she gave birth to him. Joseph was, for all intents and purpose, the foster father to Jesus, not a blood relative. So why do the writers trace Jesus' genealogy through Joseph?

The second problem is that the genealogies are different. In Matthew, Joseph's father is Jacob. In Luke it is Heli.

The third is that while Matthew traces Joseph's lineage starting with Abraham, the father of the Jews, through King David to Joseph, Luke's genealogy goes from Joseph all the way back to Adam, the father of the human race. With a little help from the Internet, I can trace my lineage back to the clan of Ripley Castle in Yorkshire, England in the 17th century. To trace a lineage back to Adam in the Garden of Eden is an amazing genealogy, to say the least.

There are many other passages in the gospels whose origins are questionable. As much as it is a moving moment, the story of Jesus forgiving the woman caught in adultery shouldn't be in the Bible at all. It is not in the earliest and best manuscripts of the gospel of John. It does not appear in any Greek manuscript until the fifth century, and no Greek church father comments on the passage before the 12th century.

Much to my dismay, I found that when you take the Bible seriously as a source book, you discover that entire empires and rigorous traditions have been erected on the flimsiest textual foundations. For instance, the entire ecclesial structure of the Roman Catholic Church is based on one verse, Matthew 16:18-19, where Jesus says to Simon, *"You are Peter and upon this rock I will build my church ... I will give you the keys of the kingdom of heaven."* Mark and John say Jesus gave Simon the name Peter (the Greek noun petros or rock), but Matthew is the only gospel that adds an explanation for Jesus giving the name. Let's just say that for scholars, it smacks of a later addition.

What ever happened to Peter? In the Acts of the Apostles he fades out halfway into the book when we are told: "he departed and went to another place" (Acts 12:17). The spotlight then shifts to Paul.

While St. Peter's Basilica in Rome is alleged to be built over Peter's grave, there is no evidence in the New Testament that Peter ever went to Rome. In the last chapter of Paul's letter to the Romans around 58 CE, he gives a long list of those to whom he sends greetings. Peter is not among them.

- 53 -

Only twice in all four gospels, and only in Matthew, do we find the word church (ecclesia in Greek or literally "called out ones"). There is no indication anywhere else that Jesus was thinking of founding a church when he was assembling his 12 disciples.

The resurrection of Jesus is undoubtedly the pinnacle of the Christian story. When the women go to the tomb to anoint the body, do they meet one man (as Mark says), two men (as Luke says), or an angel (as Matthew says)? We can say these are merely details and given the years of oral history the differences are easy to understand. But they present a challenge to the notion that the Bible is without error.

What happened? We just don't know. What we do know from the biblical record itself is that stories of resurrection were practically commonplace at that time. Lazarus was raised from death. So was Jairus' daughter. St. Matthew's gospel tells us that when Jesus died, graves were opened and the dead came walking out and made their way into Jerusalem (Matthew 27:52,53).

As for improbabilities, at his trial Jesus chats with Pontius Pilate. It's unlikely that Pilate would have known the Semitic language of Aramaic and unlikely Jesus of Nazareth, the carpenter's son, would have spoken Latin. How did they communicate? Did they have a translator? I was encountering the ambiguity of the gospels in that the more you know, the less you know. Let me point out once again that the inconsistencies and improbabilities are not in themselves arguments against the existence of God, but they kept punching holes in my rock-solid conviction that the Bible was somehow inspired by God.

What about the rest of the New Testament? The book of Acts is an account from the second half of the first century telling of the spread of Christianity. Much of the book consists of the speeches of Peter in the first third of the book and Paul in the final two-thirds. Many of these speeches give us early views of Jesus. Rather than being the pre-existing Son of God as suggested in the gospel of John written later, Jesus is depicted as coming into existence when he is born of a virgin, or when he is baptized, or when he begins his public ministry or when God raised him from the dead.[10]

As for Paul, he is the earliest Christian writer. Paul did not compose a gospel. What he wrote were letters to Christians to deal with problems that had come up in the early Church. So what does Paul tell us about Jesus? Not much.

He was born a male Jew. He had brothers. He was a descendent of David with a mission to the Jews. Other than referring to a tradition he received about Jesus at the Last Supper (1 Corinthians 11:22-24), Jesus' teaching on divorce and on whether apostles have a right to be supported financially, Paul gives us scant narrative on the life of Jesus. Again, this should not be too surprising because he's writing to Christians who have already heard and, we might assume, accepted that Jesus is the Messiah.

What this was suggesting to me, however, was that while these earliest writings assume that Jesus existed and was crucified, details of his life appear only later with the emergence of gospels.

What do we learn about Jesus from those outside the widening circle of Christian believers? Unfortunately, no Greek or Roman author from the first century mentions Jesus. You might think that if there was someone who was performing miracles and raising the dead in the first century, it might get a mention. To be fair, however, we shouldn't be surprised that there are no eyewitness accounts of Jesus either from the gospels or from outside the gospels. Hardly anyone could write and the writings of those who could have not survived. We don't have writings about the rule of Pontius Pilate even though, as Roman governor of Judea for 10 years between 26 and 36 CE, he would have been immensely significant to the history of Palestine during Jesus' adult life. He most certainly existed (we have some coins issued during his reign), even though we have few records.

Within a hundred years of the traditional date of Jesus' death, three Roman authors mention Jesus. Pliny the Elder was a Roman governor who wrote to the Roman emperor Trajan about Christians who were meeting in the mornings who would "sing hymns to Christ as to a god." A Roman biographer, Suetonius, suggested that during the reign of Claudius, he deported Jews from Rome because of riots that occurred "at the instigation of Chrestus." A Roman historian, Tacitus, tells us that when Rome burned, Emperor Nero put the blame on Christians and then had them rounded up and executed.

As for Jewish references to Jesus, there is a passage in the writing of Flavius Josephus that talks about Jesus. The problem here is that the description is something only a Christian would write, suggesting that it was inserted by believing scribes copying the text.

In short, the material we have, both from the gospels themselves, as well as the writings of Paul and others outside the Christian faith, clearly suggests there was a Jesus of Nazareth but they are not helpful as historical documents.

So I had to make a decision. Was there a Jesus of Nazareth? There is no historical evidence. We have no Golgotha or Garden Tomb except for the places invented in 325 CE by St. Helen, the mother of Constantine. There are vague references in the writings of Flavius Josephus and Tacitus, but in copies made centuries after the crucifixion.

There are some who say there never was a Jesus of Nazareth, that he was a complete myth invented by early Christians. I don't agree, for two reasons. First of all, why go through the literary gymnastics to get Jesus' parents from an inconspicuous hamlet called Nazareth to the City of David at the time of his birth if he hadn't come from there? Why not just have him born in Bethlehem without bothering with a fabricated census of the entire Roman Empire?

Secondly, Jesus thought God was going to intervene within his generation to destroy the forces of evil and set up a new kingdom. "Truly I say to you, there are some of those who are standing here who shall not taste of death until they see the kingdom of God after it has come with power" (Mark 9:1). Elsewhere he says that the events of the end will happen before "this generation" passes away (Mark 13:30, Matthew 24:34). He warns his listeners to be on their guard, suggesting that the end was coming soon and they should be prepared (Mark 13:33-37).

As it turned out, Jesus was wrong. Why include his prediction in the gospels if it ended up not happening?

In short, I was becoming increasingly convinced that the Jesus of history was not the Jesus of the Bible; that he has evolved into a Jesus of our imagination, our invention, to meet our needs and serve our causes. I can't stress enough how disconcerting this was to someone who had always assumed and believed that Jesus was the one true manifestation of the God who made the universe and who made me.

I felt Jesus of Nazareth was not a total fabrication. He was a Jew of first-century Palestine. But I was quickly adopting the view that Jesus was an apocalyptic preacher; the view first advanced by Albert Schweitzer. The word "apocalyptic" comes from the Greek word *apocalypsis*, which means a revealing or unveiling. Apocalypticism emerged in Jewish thinking long before Jesus appeared. Judea had been under the control of foreign powers for centuries – Babylonians, Persians, Greeks and Syrians. Where Jewish prophets had proclaimed in the century and a half before Jesus appeared that their nation was suffering at God's hand because of their disobedience, many Jews were turning back to God and following the Torah. Jewish apocalyptic notions arose that their suffering was not a punishment for sin but for righteousness, a punishment inflicted by the forces of evil that were against God.

The view emerged that God was about to crash into history to destroy the forces of evil, vindicate his people, restore them to a place of privilege and usher in a new kingdom that would last forever. To do this, God would send a divine saviour from heaven. Some called him a messiah. Others referred to him as the Son of Man based on the book of Daniel, the last book of the Hebrew Bible written around 165 BCE. The rich and the powerful who had sided with the forces of evil would be destroyed when the Son of Man arrived. The weak, the poor and the oppressed would be vindicated. There would be a resurrection of the dead and a final judgement. Most Jews thought that after death, a person continued to live in a shadowy netherworld called Sheol or they simply died. But apocalypticists believed in a future eternal life for the righteous in the coming Kingdom of God that would soon arrive.

There was apocalyptic fever in the air of first-century Palestine. Fire-breathing prophets and liberating messiahs were everywhere. Some are even named in the Bible. According to the book of Acts, a prophet named Theudas had four hundred disciples before Rome cut his head off (Acts 5:36). In 4 BCE, a shepherd named Athronges put a diadem on his head and crowned himself "King of the Jews"; he and his followers were brutally cut down by a legion of solders. There was Hezekiah the bandit chief, Simon of Peraea, Judas the Galilean, his grandson Menahem, Simon son of Giora and Simon son of Kochba. Another messianic aspirant, called simply "the Samaritan," was crucified by Pontius Pilate even though he raised no army and in no way challenged Rome—an indication that the authorities had become extremely sensitive to any hint of sedition.[11]

Jesus believed in the forces of evil and considered the Roman Empire party to those forces. He believed in the coming apocalypse when God would destroy the present kingdom and set up a new kingdom on the earth. He believed that this cataclysmic end of history would come in his own generation, or at least during the lifetime of his disciples (Mark 9:1). The record of Jesus attacking traders in the Temple in Jerusalem and his remarks about his teaching offering strife and division seem to reflect this revolutionary aspect to his personality.[12]

What we notice in the New Testament is that by the time we get to the gospel of John, the last of the four canonical accounts, Jesus doesn't talk about a coming Kingdom of God but eternal life that is available here and now to the believer. The apocalyptic message about a coming kingdom has been muted and replaced with an emphasis on faith in Jesus, who gives eternal life beginning now. This theme carries on into the second century in the Coptic gospel of Thomas, a collection of 114 secret teachings of Jesus discovered in 1945 when peasants digging for fertilizer near the village of Nag Hammadi in Egypt accidentally uncovered a jar with 13 leather-bound manuscripts. This gospel seems to attack those who believe in a future kingdom. In teaching #3, Jesus says that the kingdom is "within you and outside you."[13] The Kingdom of God will not break into history but rather is salvation available to all who place their faith in him. The message of Jesus evolved within the gospels themselves.

What then would take a common apocalyptic preacher like Jesus and have him morph into the eternal creator of the universe manifest in human form who would die and rise again? To answer this question, I looked beyond the gospels to the pagan religions before and during the life of Jesus. I learned, to my dismay, that the story of Christianity is hardly original. Life in the first century was rife with notions of virgin births and resurrections. From the Egyptian vegetation myths mirroring the crops that die in winter and come back to life in spring, to tales of heroes who went down to and returned from the underworld (some like Hercules achieving apotheosis or elevation to divine status), gods regularly died and rose again.

As for archetypes for a saviour, we find them in Dionysus, Osiris, Adonis, Mithras, Krishna, Buddha, Hercules and even Plato and Pythagoras.

Consider the close similarities, if not direct parallels, between Osiris and Horus in Egyptian mythology and the Christ of the gospels. Horus, the divine son, "left the courts of heaven"[14] and descended to Earth. He was born of a virgin, became a substitute for humanity, went down to Hades to bring life to the dead, the "first fruits" to lead the resurrected into the life to come. St. Paul talked about Jesus as the "first fruits" of the resurrection. As farmers gather in the first fruits of the harvest and then go on to harvest the rest of the crop, Jesus' resurrection is the first of all of those who have died and will face God's judgement.

Slaves and women would naturally be attracted to the promise of Herculean apotheosis through faith, setting them free, albeit posthumously, from the chains of oppression and rewarding them for their suffering.

Jesus is then, for me, a mythic legend. In tales of supernatural beings, ancestors or heroes, myths attempt to explain the reasons why things are as they are, the seasons and the stars, for instance. There are creation myths to spell out how we got here and myths to explain natural phenomena like earthquakes and thunder. We don't need myths now to explain the natural world. We know why there are seasons and tides and stars and storms.

A legend is a story handed down through generations, told as if it is historical but without evidence. When you step back and look at how the New Testament came to us, how beliefs about Jesus evolved and continue to evolve, it appeared more and more to me that the figure of Jesus the Christ is similar to Robin Hood or St. Nicholas. All were historical figures on whom the aspirations and imaginations of generations layered legendary folklore. I simply could not escape the notion that the miracle-working, wind-corralling, resurrected Jesus is an amalgam of fact and fantasy that creates a legendary figure.

At the same time, the fully developed story of Jesus in the Bible serves as a mythology to give some explanation to questions about where we came from and why things happen. Jesus is the creator of everything and, as the song goes, has the whole world in his hands; a mythic legend.

Time for a deep breath. When I was a believer, it was disconcerting to be told there are mistakes in the Bible; that the gospels were written decades after Jesus' death; that they were written in Greek, which Jesus and his disciples didn't speak or write if they could write at all; and that they were written to fit a prophecy more than narrate a profile. It was something I just didn't want to face. It didn't fit my faith. Not once in 35 years did I preach a sermon about evidence for the historic Jesus. I never considered it important. I needed to comfort the afflicted and afflict the comfortable, but never did I see it as important to talk about the skepticism of biblical scholarship.

I'll be the first to admit that to a believing Christian, it was and is distressing to hear that following years of a fluid oral tradition, and without original writings, all we have are fragments of copies of copies of copies made over centuries by some scribes who may have made intentional alterations to make the text say what either they wanted it to say or thought it should say. If many of the books in the Bible were not written by Jesus' inner circle at all, but by writers living decades later with different agendas in rival communities, what does that do to the authority of scripture? What is more likely, that tales told from generation to generation over centuries would naturally morph and mutate, or that God would tell an unerring but internally inconsistent tale to illiterate Bronze Age herdsmen and first-century fishermen?

As I confronted what we know about the Bible and other religions, it was evident to me that the scriptures are no more the inerrant inspired word of God than those of Persian fables or Icelandic sagas. If I easily dismiss the tales of Osiris, Mithras and Hercules as fabrications, why would I readily accept the nearly identical story of Jesus of Nazareth? If, say, I had been born in a time and in a culture that revered Osiris, would I have entered into the ministry and possibly become the head priest of the largest mainline temple of the day? If someone had come to my door and gladly shared the good news about Hercules, would I have turned them away because obviously the story of Hercules is a fable? Or would I have been captivated by the story of this new deity and abandoned my faith in Osiris? Is what we believe more the result of when and where we are born than the objective truth of the belief? These and other questions were propelling me farther and farther in my sojourn.

Even though I was newly convinced that the Jesus of history bears little resemblance to the Christ adored in church, there was something else that had troubled me for a long time. It was the obvious dichotomy between a first-century homeless, penniless vagabond apocalyptic preacher and the pomp and power of geopolitical Christendom.

I needed to revisit my church history. I did. It isn't pretty.

[8] CE (Common Era or Christian Era) is an alternative naming of the traditional calendar era, Anno Domini "in the Year of Our Lord", abbreviated AD

[9] Bart D. Ehrman, *Peter, Paul, and Mary Magdalene : The Followers of Jesus in History and Legend* (Oxford; New York: Oxford University Press, 2006), xii-xiii.

[10] This view doesn't come from Paul, but is in an early creed that Paul quotes at the beginning of his letter to the Romans 1:3,4.

[11] Reza Aslan, *Zealot : The Life and Times of Jesus of Nazareth, First Edition*. ed. (New York: Random House, 2013), 4.

[12] Matthew 10:34 comes to mind. "Do not think that I came to bring peace on the Earth; I did not come to bring peace, but a sword."

[13] Bart D. Ehrman, *Lost Scriptures: Books That Did Not Make It into the New Testament* (New York: Oxford University Press, 2003), 20.

[14] Tom Harpur, *The Pagan Christ : Recovering the Lost Light* (New York: Walker & Co., 2005), 89.

CHAPTER FIVE

· KILLING FOR CHRIST ·

Tantum religio potuit suadere malorum.
(To such heights of evil are men driven by religion.)
Lucretius, De Rerum Natura

Politics has slain its thousands, but religion has slain its tens of thousands.
Sean O'Casey

My wife and I were captivated by the first season of the television series *The Borgias*, starring Jeremy Irons as Rodrigo Borgia or Pope Alexander VI. Dubbed "the original crime family," at first I couldn't believe that this pope, this vicar of Christ, this allegedly infallible interpreter of divine revelation, this link in the apostolic chain from St. Peter to the current Pope, was portrayed as thoroughly amoral and corrupt. My research confirmed that, in fact, he was!

Some of my Roman Catholic friends may be dismayed that I am focused on their tradition more than the Protestant tradition from which I emerged. My response is that until the Reformation in the 16th century, the Roman Church was, for all practical purposes, the face of Christianity. Even today, given its scope and power, the face of organized religion for most non-believers is the Roman Catholic church. The Protestant face of Christianity is hardly angelic, but I'll come that shortly.

I began to delve into the history of the papacy and the consolidations of its power and wealth. Since the third century, when Christianity became the official religion of the Roman Empire, the scope of the Church has continually expanded.

At the same time, church leaders were preoccupied with forging and enforcing a set of beliefs against many "heresies" or views different from their own. I was aghast at the vandalism against knowledge and books, rooted in the notion that learning hinders access to God. The Arian and Athanasian Christians, who differed in their understanding of the relationship between God the Father and God the Son Jesus Christ, persecuted and killed each other even after the Roman Empire made Christianity the state religion in 325 CE.

Donatists were Christians in North Africa who claimed, among other things, that the effectiveness of the sacraments depends on the moral character of the minister. In other words, if a minister who was involved in a serious enough sin were to baptize a person, that baptism would be considered invalid. Donatists declared themselves to be the true church against the Catholic Church, which made the claim for itself. Non-believers might just shake their heads at the apparent foolishness of the issues splitting early Christians but these believers were earnest and prepared to fight and die for the doctrinal positions they held.

What troubled me the most in revisiting church history, however, was the level of violence and corruption that has always been a part of religion, and Christianity in particular, beginning with the machinations of Emperor Constantine to co-opt this fledgling faith and in the following years, to use it to consolidate wealth and power. In 321, Constantine declared the Church was qualified to hold and transmit property. According to papal historian John Julius Norwich, by the time of Pope Gregory the Great (590-604) the Church was the largest single landowner in Western Europe.[15]

For the next thousand years, tithes poured in from all over Europe. Non-Christians and even fellow Christians were murdered and their property confiscated. The Fourth Crusade and the sack of Constantinople in the early 13th century, for example, were an opportune source of gold, cash and jewels. I was not unaware of the violence and greed that mark the first thousand years of Christianity. But now that I had read of a God who had no compunction about killing babies and who told his chosen people to kill all their enemies but keep the gold for the treasury, I was seeing the followers of this deity doing the same thing—engaging in genocide and acquiring lots and lots of property in the process. More and more it seemed to me that instead of God creating us in His image, we have created a god in our image.

Despite the campaign to create and enforce a unifying set of beliefs, the quarrels of Christianity brought about the first major schism when the Roman and Byzantine versions parted company in the eighth century.

A second, and I would say more consequential, schism occurred in the 16th century. German monk Martin Luther nailed a list of theses for debate to a church door in Wittenberg, Germany in 1517. He was protesting against the practice of selling indulgences where you could reduce your time in purgatory (the posthumous place where your soul will be purged of its sins) by paying money to the Church. The Reformation sparked by Luther brought more than a century of terrible violence. The Thirty Years War, fought largely as a religious conflict between Protestants and Catholics between 1618 and 1648, caused the death of one in every three of the German-speaking peoples of Europe.

The protesting (hence the word "Protestant") communities split into Lutheran and Calvinist denominations. The schisms have spawned thousands of sects. According to the *World Christian Encyclopedia* compiled by by David B. Barrett, George T. Kurian, and Todd M. Johnson (2001 edition), there are over 33,000 Protestant denominations.[16] Many of them are convinced that all the others are, in some ways, wrong.

Of course nobody, not even Jesus of Nazareth, could have expected the Spanish Inquisition. Sadly, the Inquisition was not just a blip on the radar to give comedic fodder to Mel Brooks and Monty Python. Instead, it was a Chapter of church history that lasted for 600 years. It began in 1184 to crush a movement called Catharism, which was an unorthodox belief about this world and Jesus. Cathars were dualists who believed that there were two Gods—the good God of the spiritual world and the Bad God of the material world. Cathars also severely criticized the worldliness and corruption of the Catholic Church. But heresy is heresy and if you believe that the Bible is the infallible Word of God, then the heretic must die. In 1199 Pope Innocent lll decreed that all property belonging to a convicted heretic would be forfeited to the church.

But the practice for which the Inquisition is most famous, and infamous, is the use of torture to extract confessions from the accused. I find it painful to even contemplate the horrors of the techniques the Church used to coerce confessions from alleged heretics. I cringe at the sight of the instruments of torture used in the name of Jesus: the Confession Chair; the Iron Maiden; the Strappado or Palestinian hanging. Even St. Augustine said heretics should be tortured. St. Thomas Aquinas felt they should be killed.

Protestant readers should not be smug for a second. German Reformer Martin Luther advocated the murder of not only heretics but Jews and witches too. Pope Innocent III said, "Anyone who attempts to construe a personal view of God which conflicts with Church dogma must be burned without pity."

In southern Europe in the 13th century the Church engaged in its own acts of terrorism to threaten heretical groups such as the Cathars, burning 200 of them in an enormous pyre. I had to ask myself how pious Church leaders could find the justification to torture and burn innocent people because their understanding of Christianity did not conform to the precise doctrines of the day.

No one was safe in those days. Giordano Bruno, an Italian Dominican friar, philosopher, mathematician and astronomer, was imprisoned for seven years and then executed in 1600 because he agreed with Copernicus that the Earth revolved around the sun.

During the Inquisition, if you admitted to your torturers that you were indeed a heretic or a witch, you would have to confirm your story before the judge. If you repented of your sins, these compassionate and learned men of the Church would do you the kindness of strangling you before lighting your funeral pyre. As I said, the Inquisition lasted for six centuries.

This is not piety. This is madness.

The Spanish Inquisition only stopped persecuting heretics in 1834. The last sentencing was in 1850 in Mexico, about the time Charles Darwin set sail in the Beagle. While we might like to think this practice has been abolished, the Supreme Sacred Congregation of the Roman and Universal Inquisition, which Pope Paul III established in 1542, exists today as the Congregation for the Doctrine of the Faith (Congregatio pro Doctrina Fidei).

While Christianity, thankfully, has stopped killing heretics, Islam has kept the practice alive. Tragically, there are Islamic countries where people are stoned or beheaded for the imaginary crime of blasphemy. Sunni and Shia Muslims are killing one another every day. And as we well know, particularly since 9/11, Islamic jihadists are eager to utter the words *Allahu akbar* (God is Great) and proceed to end their lives in the hope of ending the lives of non-believers.

It is argued that you should not judge a religion by its extremists and it is true that not all people of faith are prone to violence. Unfortunately, however, religious extremists are the tail wagging the dog. They are intent on bringing fear into our hearts and disruption into our daily lives and are doing a good job at both.

Returning to Christianity, Protestants cannot claim innocence. Protestantism stems from the protests of Martin Luther, the Catholic priest who called into question some of the basic tenets of the Roman Catholic Church. He objected to the sale of indulgences to raise money to rebuild St. Peter's Cathedral in Rome. He also thought that individuals could seek salvation on their own, without relying on priests. His sentiments, intended to provoke debate, became public when some unknown person reprinted Luther's writings in a pamphlet that was eventually distributed throughout Germany.

His refusal to retract his writings at the demand of Pope Leo X in 1520 and Emperor Charles V in 1521 led to his excommunication by the Pope and condemnation as an outlaw by the emperor. His followers soon split from the Roman Catholic Church to begin the Protestant tradition.

What is less well known, however, is that in 1543 Luther published *On the Jews and Their Lies*, a 65,000-word anti-Semitic treatise in which he said that the Jews are full of the "devil's feces ... which they wallow in like swine." The synagogue was a "defiled bride, yes, an incorrigible whore and an evil slut..." He argued that their synagogues and schools be set on fire, their prayer books destroyed, rabbis forbidden to preach, homes razed and property and money confiscated. They should be shown no mercy or kindness, afforded no legal protection, and these "poisonous envenomed worms" should be drafted into forced labor or expelled for all time.[17] He also seemed to advocate their murder, writing in Chapter 14 of his essay, "We are even at fault in not avenging all this innocent blood of our Lord and of the Christians which they shed for three hundred years after the destruction of Jerusalem, and the blood of the children they have shed since then (which still shines forth from their eyes and their skin). We are at fault in not slaying them."

To be fair, Luther's harsh anti-Jewish statements have been repudiated in recent years. Since the 1980s, some Lutheran Church bodies have formally denounced and dissociated themselves from Luther's writings on the Jews.

The prevailing view among historians, however, is that Luther's rhetoric contributed significantly to the development of anti-Semitism in Germany, and in the 1930s and 1940s, provided an ideal foundation for the Nazi Party's attempt to systematically eliminate Jews.

While repudiation of Luther's views on the Jews may make it more palatable to accept his other writings, it does pose a quandary. We might look back at Luther and say he was writing in a different time and said some things we now reject, even as there are other things we still accept. But Luther is considered by some to be God's messenger, and if this reasoned explanation is acceptable to the Church, why do we then accept everything that found its way into the Bible, including things that are as horrific as Luther's views on the Jews? If we accept that God's relatively recent messengers are subject to bouts of self-interested insanity, which we are free to reject, why don't we hold ancient messengers to the same standards? Is it because the messengers are more ancient or their cultures more distant from ours? Or is it because Church leaders have decided some messengers of God have more legitimacy than others? On what grounds?

We would like to think that in a modern moral zeitgeist, where we abhor religious violence, killing someone else in the name of a God of love and peace would be a thing of the past, that the clarion call for religious tolerance would have all but drowned out the fanatical cries of animosity. Alas, that is not the case. Under the pretext of nationalism, sectarian warfare in Ireland between Catholics and Protestants has left the streets of Belfast in ruins. From there to Beirut to Baghdad, believers are making history by keeping old hatreds alive and occasionally acting on them, creating havoc in the name of a deity of peace: Jews and Muslims in Palestine; Muslims and Hindus in Kashmir; Muslims and Christians in Nigeria; Buddhists and Hindus in Sri Lanka; Shiite and Sunni Muslims in Iran and Iraq. As American physicist and Nobel laureate Steven Weinberg said in a speech in Washington, D.C. in 1999, "With or without religion, you would have good people doing good things and evil people doing evil things. But for good people to do evil things, that takes religion."[18]

What is it about belief that motivates violence? What is in faith that can turn otherwise level-headed individuals to commit monstrous acts of cruelty, not only toward heretics or those of other faiths, but to those who profess no faith at all?

Some seek to kill others because they are convinced God wants them to do it. The infidel must die. But, as neuroscientist Sam Harris points out, far greater numbers of people fall into conflict with one another because they define their moral community on the basis of their religious affiliation.[19] Instead of being knit together in bonds of peace, societies have been fragmented by religious bigotry, fuelling prejudice and reactionary thinking. Religious tales have been manufactured to fit our human interests, aspirations and needs. Those tales have been taken by charlatans to line their pockets and fuel their private jets and keep them on television to continue to ask for money. It's a vicious and vile circle.

So much for the institution of religion, but what about individual believers? What about the wonderful people I knew in my ministry? What about all the lovely ladies who worked tirelessly to provide refreshments after funeral services or make church suppers to raise money for the congregation? What about all the kindhearted souls who remembered me at Christmas with copious baked goods and baskets of fruits and jams? What about all of my dear Christian friends? Surely they are a testimony to the power of faith to make people good. Does religion make people better? I asked this question many times over years of working with believers from all walks of life in all kinds of situations. I was asking it again.

---

[15] John Julius Norwich, *Absolute Monarchs : A History of the Papacy*, 1st U.S. ed. (New York: Random House, 2011), 43.

[16] The 2001 edition, successor to the 1982 first edition, identifies 10,000 distinct religions, of which 150 have 1 million or more followers. Within Christianity, they count 33,820 denominations.

[17] Luther, Martin. *On the Jews and Their Lies*, Trans. Martin H. Bertram, in *Luther's Works*. (Philadelphia: Fortress Press, 1971).

[18] http://www.physlink.com/Education/essay_weinberg.cfm

[19] Sam Harris, *Letter to a Christian Nation*, 1st Vintage Books ed. (New York: Vintage Books, 2008), 81.

CHAPTER SIX

· GOOD FOR GOD'S SAKE ·

You don't need a reason to help people.
Anonymous

I'm an atheist, and that's it. I believe there's nothing we can know except
that we should be kind to each other and do what we can for each other.
Katharine Hepburn

As you might suspect, after working within institutional Christianity for almost 35 years, I'm familiar with the appalling politics of religion. I've watched people manoeuvre into positions of power and then use those positions to promote their particular agenda or crush a particular enemy, not unlike the world outside religion. I've had my share of anonymous venomous letters and voice-mail messages, cloaked by a shroud of piety. I'd quote them here but I made it a practice a few years ago to delete/destroy missives whose writers were too cowardly to identify themselves.

What about the run-of-the-mill believer? What about the soul who goes to church somewhat regularly, helps out when asked and tries to muddle through life somehow? I've known good people who are Christians and bad people who are Christians. I've also known good people who are not Christians and bad people who are not Christians. The question I wrestled with of late is whether believing in God makes someone more likeable or at least more worthy of being liked. Among my three dearest male friends are Orville, Kim and Dan. Each is a committed Christian. Knowing them and loving them the way I do, however, I suspect they'd be great loveable guys even if they weren't Christians. On the other hand, I once had a person on the staff of a church I served who had a "religious experience" while she worked with us. Unfortunately, the closer she got to Jesus, the less the rest of the staff wanted to be around her.

Unlike those who adopt the view that Christians should only associate with fellow believers, I've never felt bound by such an edict. In fact, over the years I've enjoyed relationships with folks outside the faith as much as those of the faith. I've said so publicly. In sermons over the years I've mentioned that, in many ways, if looking for authenticity and curiosity and hospitality, I'd rather hang around the sinners than the saints. Jesus was notorious for doing that. "And it happened that as He was reclining at table in the house, behold many tax-gatherers and sinners came and joined Jesus and His disciples at the table" (Matthew 9:10). To put it in my context, I concluded a long time ago that there is no direct correlation between the Christian faith and people I like.

Of course Christians should be good. "For it is written; You shall be holy, for I am holy" (1 Peter 1:16). Or as we sing in the hymn *Once in Royal David's City*, "Christian children all must be, kind, obedient, good as He".

Why should a Christian be good? Is it because goodness is intrinsically good? Is it because they want to emulate Jesus and follow in his steps? Or is it because they are commanded to be good and threatened with punishment if they are not? If that is the case, then what good is being good if it is merely a means to a heavenly end?

The notion I grew up with and, to some extent carried into adulthood, is that I/we had better watch out because we are being watched all the time. One of the first songs I learned in Sunday School went like this:

O be careful little eyes what you see (repeat)
For the Father up above, is watching down below
So be careful little eyes what you see.

O be careful little ears what you hear...

O be careful little hands what you do... [20]

The popular conviction, in this song and elsewhere, is that God is observing every human being 24/7 and those who believe in a watchful God are allegedly on their best behaviour under the threat of punishment for bad behaviour. Again, this begs the question of whether you are being good because there's a reward for it (or conversely a penalty for not being good), rather than being good for goodness' sake?

Some people figure that even if they've been less than moral (which includes, well, everyone) they can ask forgiveness, get absolution and be rewarded with heaven. Am I sorry because I messed up or am I sorry because I might burn in hell if I don't fess up to my mess?

But apart from the issues of what motivates individual behaviour, there is the much broader and murkier topic of religious morals and ethics.

What I have found fascinating in this journey toward atheism is that religious folks appear to have a hard time imagining how an atheist could be good. Or even want to be good. Those without faith are deemed by those with faith to also be without ethics. The notion "if God does not exist, then everything is permitted" is (mis)attributed to Dostoyevsky's *The Brothers Karamazov* to bolster the notion that people justify bad behaviour in the non-existence of God. Perhaps some do.

What I have also found is that the opposite notion is more common; that "because God exists, everything is permitted." The vilest human behaviour is justified with the qualification that it is done in God's name or stems from God's favour. The Jewish notion of being a chosen people has historically vindicated expropriation of land and violence toward those who owned the land. The Jesus who is alleged to come bearing a sword instead of peace (Matthew 10:34) has given justification to the Crusades, the Inquisition, the Thirty Years War, the English Civil War, the conquest of the Mayans, the Aztecs and the Inca, periodic pogroms against the Jews, ethnocide and colonialism of native North Americans. The list is long.

The Quran calls on Muslims to destroy not only unbelievers but also "People of the Book" [21], all in the name of a merciful God, of course. What is permitted, it seems, is the slaughter of anyone whom God (Yahweh, Allah or Jesus) tells us to kill, based on our interpretation of holy writ or a voice we hear in our heads or hearts.

And still, people of faith maintain that their God-given morality is somehow superior. How so? Well, because God says so. Their ethics are based on what God requires or prohibits. If God commands it, it must be right. If God forbids it, it must be wrong. Socrates asked, "Is conduct right because the gods command it, or do the gods command it because it is right?"[22]

If we say that our morality is based on what God commands, God could ask us to do something horrible simply by declaring the horrible act to be good. A brief look at the ways of Yahweh reveal commands for actions such as infanticide from which we today rightfully recoil.

Theists will be quick to suggest that not all atheists are nice people. Some are nice, but certainly not all. Throughout my 25 years as a weekly syndicated columnist, I would once in a while receive an email from someone lambasting me for my Christian faith in a way that was insulting and degrading. I didn't appreciate it then and I wouldn't appreciate it now. Just because someone doesn't believe in God, it doesn't mean he is, if you'll pardon the metaphor, an angel.

Are atheists obnoxious because they are atheists? I don't think so. Remember my three dear friends? I think of them as great guys who are also Christians. Another dear friend is not a Christian. He's a great guy who is also an atheist. It all comes down to personal character. It is wrong to use broad strokes to paint believers as nice and non-believers as nasty, partly because we associate their opinions about God with their behaviours. It is never so simple. For instance, I smile when I hear theists so anxious to point out the 20th century horrors of dastardly dictators by pointing to Adolph Hitler, whose army wore the words "Gott Mit Uns" (God with us) on their belt buckles.

I also smile when I hear religious folks decry the non-believers' lack of a religious absolute morality. What would that religious absolute morality entail? The stoning of adulterers? The killing of apostates? Slavery? Genocide? Repression of women?

There is a godless ethic. There is a morality outside religion. There have been stable societies throughout human history who have punished murder and theft quite apart from any supernatural edict. Scandinavian countries, which are not known for their religious fervour, have crime rates per capita far lower than, say, the United States, where religious fervour is practically a national treasure.

I don't want a morality based on some alleged revelation but on criteria that are measured and thoughtful. I want a morality born from the experience of humans living together, where they have learned and concluded that they have to adjust their own conduct, considering the claims and needs of others. I don't like pain, other than the self-inflicted kind that comes from training to run marathons, which has an obvious physiological role. So I should not do anything that unnecessarily inflicts pain on others. I like it when someone does something nice for me, so I should strive to do nice things for others. I know how naive and simplistic this ethic of reciprocity sounds, but there is no mystery to morality and it need not be overly complex. What if we all just lived by the Golden Rule or its equivalent in other cultures and contexts?

By now I was convinced that the Bible, rather than being a guidebook for good morals and ethics, is merely a text from which people can justify their own evil or good. If that is the case, if the use of the Bible comes down to the pre-existing morality of the reader, then what's the use of the text in the first place? It was clear to me that alleged holy writ provides ample fodder to support acts people want to pursue in the first place, from oppressing women and homosexuals and killing infidels to doing acts of charity and grace. If bad people point to the Bible as the inspiration for their malevolent deeds, they were likely bad people in the first place. If good people point to the Bible as their inspiration, my hunch is that they were good people before they read the Bible. For me, the, the Bible was not only not inspired by a deity but less and less an ultimate source of morality.

For example, Christians admire the Ten Commandments as an exemplary moral code for society because they forbid stealing and murder and such. But ask any decent person to come up with their own 10 commandments, and I would venture to guess you'd find a code of conduct more helpful to humanity than anything carved into tablets on Mount Sinai.

To give just one example, British philosopher A. C. Grayling has compiled distillations of the wisdom and experience of humankind under 14 constituent parts that resemble the Bible in structure: Genesis, Wisdom, Parables, Concord, Lamentations, Consolations, Sages, Songs, Histories, Proverbs, The Lawgiver, Acts, Epistles and The Good. In the final section, The Good, Grayling has compiled a secular version of he Ten Commandments.[23]

1. Love well.

2. Seek the good in all things.

3. Harm no others.

4. Think for yourself.

5. Take responsibility.

6. Respect nature.

7. Do your utmost.

8. Be informed.

9. Be kind.

10. Be courageous.

I would vote for these mandates from Grayling's *The Good Book* to be on display in the public square for all to observe and, as much as possible, obey. At this point in my life they, more than any edicts born out of religious zeal, would make me more optimistic about the future of human behaviour.

---

[20] *O Be Careful Little Eyes What You See:* author unknown.

[21] The term "People of the Book" in the Quran refers to followers of monotheistic Abrahamic religions that are older than Islam. This includes all Christians, all Children of Israel (including Jews, Karaites and Samaritans), and Sabians.

[22] This quandary is found in Plato's *Euthyphro* and is known as the Euthypro dilemma.

[23] A. C. Grayling, *The Good Book* : A Secular Bible. p. 597

CHAPTER SEVEN

· WISHFUL THINKING ·

A sailor does not pray for wind, he learns to sail.

Gustaf Lindborg

I used to teach repeatedly that Christianity is, at its core, a relationship. Strip away all the talk of tradition and Bible and what you are left with is a bond between Jesus and you. And if you are in a relationship, any relationship, you communicate. You talk. Silence is a sign of a bond that is unhealthy at best, or non-existent at worst.

Believers talk to God and are convinced their thoughts are being heard. A lot of prayer is private. Jesus suggested that if you want a little Q and A with the Almighty, you should steal away into a secret room, shut the door and pray to the one who hears us in our secrecy (Matthew 6:6).

I talked to God most of my life. At night-time, when we four (mom, dad, brother and I) knelt down at the edge of my bed for prayers, it fell to me to light a verbal candle and offer by heart the last collect in the Anglican Book of Common Prayer for Evening Prayer, also known as Evensong:

> *Lighten our darkness, we beseech thee, O Lord; and by thy great mercy defend us from all perils and dangers of this night; for the love of thy only Son, our Saviour Jesus Christ.*

If the words sound steeped in the sixteenth century when night and day were fraught with the dangers of disease and war, they are. The language stretches back to the tenth century.

Before dinner, when it was my turn to pray, out came the prose I had committed to memory: *"For what we are about to receive, may the Lord make us truly thankful. Amen"* Looking back I'm not sure why we asked God to make us thankful. Shouldn't we have been thankful already?

By age 19, I was drawn to the less rote, more informal style of the United Church of Canada, although I am indebted to the Anglican Book of Common Prayer, which infused my ministerial vocation with a sense that not only do words matter, but their style and cadence can instill the moment with both content and dignity. Morning Prayer. Evening Prayer. Collects and Canticles.

In the enthusiasm of my late-teenaged conversion, the form of my prayers changed from rote recitations of the beautifully sculptured prose of Thomas Cranmer's Book of Common Prayer to spontaneous outbursts, the kind of chitchat you have with, well, your best friend. Jesus was my new best friend.

In the wake of my conversion I prayed more than ever before. I prayed while driving (eyes open of course). I prayed the sinner's prayer with others so that they too would have Jesus in their hearts. I prayed that someone would stop and pick me up when I hitch-hiked home from university, a prayer that would eventually be answered if I waited long enough.

In the adult vocation of ministry, prayer was part and parcel of my passion and my calling. I helped to organize city-wide prayer breakfasts with guest speakers, including evangelist Billy Graham's daughter, Anne Graham-Lotz, the Salvation Army band and representatives from a diversity of Christian denominations. I prayed at the bedside of the sick and the dying. I prayed for grieving families. I prayed for wisdom to start committee meetings and prayed at the end of the meeting, thankful for any wisdom we displayed and asking in the same breath for the fortitude to carry out any weighty decision we made before the motion to adjourn.

Most of all, I led prayer in corporate worship Sunday after Sunday. I like to think that my public prayers were an amalgam of my ardent conversion infused with the best of my Anglicanism—thoughtful preparation seasoned with spontaneity. I enjoyed wordsmithing invocations, thanksgivings and petitions to lead and guide the thoughts of the congregations I served during Sunday worship. I always felt that an economy of well-crafted public language allowed for the private fatigues of each hearer to be blended into the collective hope of the faithful.

When a big event loomed, a wedding or a church picnic, for instance, parishioners kept assuming I had a hotline to God and that my prayers would guarantee a sunny day. I was always quick to point out that I never took credit for good weather so I couldn't be blamed for bad weather. It became a standing joke.

Prayer should be personal but I rarely mentioned my parishioners' names in public prayer. The practice is fraught with danger. You can get into trouble with those you "out", who don't want the world to know about their hemorrhoids, not to mention those you don't name and feel slighted because you left them off the list of folks needing prayer. "All those who are burdened" know their burden.

I also felt prayer was debased when used to make announcements. "Lord, bless our congregation's potluck dinner tonight at 6 p.m. in the Fellowship Hall where the freewill offering will help send our young people on their mission trip this July."

I didn't pray for the dead. In one sense, talking to a dead person feels natural. A touching farewell at the funeral with "We'll miss you old guy," say, or a "Why did you have to leave me?" private lament. Such sentiments ease the pain of separation and help us work through our anger and grief.

But do the dead actually hear us? For some the veil between the quick and the dead is quite porous. In the Bible, the departed are summoned. King Saul wanted to know the outcome of the battle ahead of him. Through the medium of the witch of Endor, he dabbled in necromancy and summoned the ghost of the prophet Samuel. Samuel's news was as bad as it was true. (1 Samuel 28)

But can the dead do anything for us? This is where Christian views diverge dramatically. The Roman Catholic faithful hold to the notion that since deceased saints (and the Virgin Mary) intercede for believers, you can solicit their prayers. Protestants, not so much. But let's return to the use and misuse of prayer and whether there is, indeed, anyone hearing our wishes.

There are many forms of prayer practice. Apophatic prayer asks the devotee to still the mind and disengage from thought completely. In kataphatic prayer, believers fill their imaginations with thoughts and images from scripture, imagining Jesus carrying his cross on the Via Dolorosa, for instance.

There is also the practice of speaking in tongues, which is an alleged language thought by those who speak it as a language God knows but the speaker does not. The apostle Paul wrote about early Christians who had the gift of speaking in tongues (1 Corinthians 12:10), but it was sowing strife in the community because of its unique manifestations. Paul went on to say in the beloved chapter of 1 Corinthians 13 that the greatest gift was love. I've long been fascinated with speaking in tongues but also have known that it can be easily faked for attention. Just say "I should have bought a Hyundai" 10 times fast. Presto. You're either faking tongues for attention or worse, faking yourself out because you really want to believe you have the gift.

Of course, God gets petitions, lots and lots of petitions: for cures and directions, for succour and for just plain stuff. There is supplication (I want to land this job, Lord) and adoration (God, I'm your biggest fan).

There is the rote recitation of those who use a Prayer Book and the unison prayer of worshippers with words carefully honed by a worship leader, printed in the Sunday bulletin and read aloud together. There is also the emotive cry for help and the ecstatic cry for joy. Theologian Paul Tillich called prayer the great deep sigh. Duke Ellington said, "My music is the way I pray." Writing is the prayer of some authors. In the original manuscript, Charles Dickens ends his story of Ebenezer Scrooge with the word *Amen*. It's as if the whole story were a prayer, his prayer, a prayer that the reader would be as changed as old Ebenezer, a prayer that cold hearts would be warmed and tight fists would be open arms; that broken relationships would be mended and blind eyes opened. A beautiful heart-felt-prayer in prose.

Jesus allegedly talked about prayer and taught about prayer. The classic Lord's Prayer was his alleged response to a request for some instruction on prayer. Jesus said believers should pray and keep at it. Even a rotten parent wouldn't give a child a rock when asked for a loaf of bread, or a snake if asked for a fish, so how much more will God give to those who ask (Matthew 7:9-11).

Even when nothing happens, said Jesus, keep praying. You might wonder, then, what is the harm in praying? If events change, God must have answered the prayer. If events don't change, God must have said "No," or "Not yet." So just keep at it.

What I could no longer escape was the notion that prayer was merely wishful thinking from which we could easily discover a divine response no matter what did or did not happen. For instance, if we pray for grandma and she recovers, we rejoice that God must have heard our prayer and answered. If we pray for grandma and she dies, God heard our prayer and said "No." God chose to be merciful and took her; enfolding her in everlasting arms. It's just too easy to conclude that no matter what happens, God heard our prayerful request.

Some have tried to systematically investigate whether praying for other people is efficacious. There have been experiments where sick patients were separated into two groups, one that received prayers and another that did not. Not surprisingly, they have failed to establish any link between those who were and those who were not prayed for.

I also became more and more uncomfortable with the horrible implications of people who thank God for saving them from a tragedy. After an earthquake or tsunami where hundreds of lives are lost, people will flock to church to give thanks and pray with no sense of the irony of their intercessions. Are they thankful they were not the ones who were crushed by concrete or swept out to sea? Are they thankful that they were miraculously spared while those around them were lost? In their final moments, I can imagine the deceased prayed just as fervently that they might be spared an untimely death. So did God let some die and some live? On what basis?

Some dismiss that line of questioning with an umbrella narrative that some greater purpose had been served by the tragedy. If a terrorist is responsible for the death of hundreds, the act is considered an atrocity at the hands of a malevolent agent. But not God.

Some consider the harshness of the world as consistent with a compassionate deity by saying God's ways are not our ways. The whole thing is one great big mystery. Maybe we're being tested. Maybe the storm is a result of human sinfulness and God's punishment. Who can forget the suggestion from late evangelist Jerry Fallwell on Pat Robertson's television show that the pagans, gays, feminists and abortionists were partly responsible for the 9/11 terrorist attacks? God does work in mysterious ways.

Or consider the prayers of thanks offered by sport and entertainment celebrities when they win a game or award. As the football team bends the knee for a little pre-game intercession, if the request is for victory, then God would have to orchestrate the agony of defeat for a team of perhaps equally devout, earnest players. At the buzzer, if God helped your team win, did God do something to help the opponents lose? What if they were also praying for a victory? Did God spend time choosing which side to come up with a last-minute victory?

Did God manipulate the minds of the judges to make sure the Oscar or Emmy award went to the show or celebrity of God's choosing?

I know it sounds frivolous to ask such questions, but when people offer up prayers of gratitude to a deity, the underlying assumption is that the deity had some hand in the outcome. If survivors are convinced they had a guardian angel watching over them, you have to ask where the guardian angels were for those who perished.

For someone who once prayed without ceasing (at least it felt that way), the exercise just wasn't making any sense. Turning back to the Bible, I looked at how prayer is used in scripture and it began to upset me.

You may not have heard of imprecatory prayer. It's an ancient plea to a deity for someone else's misfortune. In the Bible, God is asked to play the hit man and zap the enemy.

David prayed it. David called upon his God to kill the enemy. Psalm 25 begins "Contend, O Lord, with those who contend with me; Fight against those who fight against me." This is not a rare dose of hyperbole or the momentary ranting of a wronged believer. The psalms were carefully crafted poems put to music for worship. They are considered the inerrant inspired word of God. Other imprecatory psalms have curses or prayers for death to one's foes.

In the Pythonesque cinematic version of the *Quest for the Holy Grail,* Arthur, king of the Britons, calls for the holy hand grenade of Antioch to vanquish a foe. Prayer is offered. "O Lord bless Thou thy hand grenade that with it Thou may'st blow Thine enemy to tiny bits, in Thy mercy." Such satire is not lost on those who are uneasy about prayerful petition for victory over the enemy.

Baptist minister and former second-vice-president of the Southern Baptist Convention, Wiley Drake offered imprecatory prayer for the death of U.S. President Barak Obama. On June 2, 2009 on Fox News Radio, Drake said of Barack Obama, "If he does not turn to God and does not turn his life around, I am asking God to enforce imprecatory prayers that are throughout the scripture that would cause him death." Pastor Drake has also called for death-dealing prayers against a religious watchdog.

How does this harsh rhetoric square with the Jesus who called for love of your enemy? It's not a case of Old Testament cursing versus New Testament loving. Proverbs 24:17 expresses a sentiment of humility when it says, "Do not gloat when your enemy falls; when he stumbles, do not let your heart rejoice." On the other hand, St. Paul, who wrote edifying New Testament letters, also wrote, "If anyone does not love the Lord, a curse be on him" (1 Corinthians 16:22). Paul may have been a saint but this is embarrassingly close to the Islamic call for death to the infidel.

Some make the case that wrathful intercession is simply asking God to do what God said he would do and protect the righteous. The danger here is in our assumption that since we're so righteous, God is always on our side. Anyone who doesn't believe what we believe and the way we believe it must be God's enemy and in line for some serious smiting, if not a death sentence.

My friend Frederick Buechner wrote, "Whatever else it may or may not be, prayer is at least talking to yourself, and that's in itself not always a bad idea. Even if you don't believe anybody's listening at least you'll be listening."[24]

I agree that at the very least, prayer is talking to yourself and talking to yourself can help to throw some light on who you are and what it is you desire most in the moment. But for people of faith, prayer is more than a healthy mental exercise. It is oil in the workings of a relationship with someone else. There is a belief that someone is listening and maybe, just maybe, making a request will have an effect. What effect? Maybe our team will win the cup. Maybe it will rain. Maybe it will stop raining. Maybe my sick friend will get well. Maybe there will be survivors of that terrible crash. The list is endless.

Prayer is offered as one reason why people believe in God. Answered prayer is considered evidence that there is a God, but I started to think of what it is people who pray are expecting. What is often hoped for is that the natural course of events, of physics or chemistry, say, will be suspended for a moment because a benevolent God either chooses to or is obliged (based on the words we use such as "In Jesus' name") to intervene just this once and grant us our wish.

If such a thing happened, that the laws of nature were temporarily suspended because I wished for it, does that prove there is a God? What about all the other religions whose followers claim that a successful hunt or good weather are proof of the existence of their deity? Hindus claim positive results of their prayers. Does it prove the existence of their gods? According to Mormons, their prayers are answered. Does this prove Jesus made an appearance in the United States?

I've titled this chapter Wishful Thinking because it now seems to me that this is the nature of prayer. It is thinking infused with wishes. Does the wishing make the wish come true? It may seem that way when it works out. It may come down to hits and misses. We don't keep track of the misses, but boy do we remember the hits! Psychics know they only have to be right a few times to be considered accurate. If a prayer is "answered" once, it seems to verify the efficacy of all prayers.

Let's be honest. If you make a lot of requests, some are bound to turn out. I get over the flu. I get a raise. The storm passes. It starts to rain. Some things turn out and some things don't. The Bible has some very clear verses on the power of prayer. *And all things, whatsoever ye shall ask in prayer, believing, ye shall receive* (Mathew 21:22). *If two of you shall agree on earth as touching anything that they shall ask, it shall be done for them of my Father which is in heaven* (Matthew 18:19) Sensible Christians know in their hearts that this isn't the way it works. And besides, what if God kept suspending the laws of nature? There would be utter chaos.

It is wonderful to think there is someone to whom you can make a wish and it will be granted. It is comforting to think someone is always working behind the scenes to make things turn out alright for you. If something bad happens, there will be a corollary, some positive consequence. For years, a Bible verse I treasured was Romans 3:23: *All things work for good to those who love God.* It was engraved on a plaque that hung in the kitchen of the manse on my first posting to serve three country churches.

But then I started thinking of the few awful things that have happened to me over the years, as they happen to all of us. If you think long enough, and creatively enough, you can find something good that came out of something bad. My wife left me, but I'm so incredibly lucky to have found the person in my life now. My mother was killed instantly by a drunk driver, but she didn't know what hit her and didn't have to suffer a long drawn-out debilitating illness. See what I mean? Despite the most horrific tragedy, in retrospect we can see some good or, as Brian Cohen and company sing while being crucified in the Monty Python film *Life of Brian*, "Always look on the bright side of life."

I mention Romans 3:23 as an example of a Bible verse that might suggest divine intervention in just about everything, but might also be considered an attitude in which anyone, believer or non-believer, can look at the events of their life. Being full of wishes and looking on the bright side are wonderful ways to live, but they have absolutely no bearing on whether or not there is a god somewhere hearing our wishes and, like the wonderful Wizard of Oz who hears the heartfelt petitions of Dorothy Gale and company, granting our requests.

---

[24] Buechner, Frederick. *Wishful Thinking : A Seeker's Abc.* Rev. and expanded ed. . ed. San Francisco, Calif.: HarperSanFrancisco, 1993, 70.

CHAPTER EIGHT

· THE STRANGE AND THE SUPERSTITIOUS ·

Faith is something that you believe
that nobody in his right mind would believe.

Archie Bunker (from the television sitcom All in the Family)

The denomination I served for more than three decades is the United Church of Canada. The doctrines of the United Church are set out in the Basis of Union, which was approved in 1925 when this grand experiment in Canadian ecumenism was first formed. It includes 20 Articles of Faith which are attempts by Christians to put down on paper what they believe in their hearts and minds about God, Jesus, the Holy Spirit, the Church, the Bible, the sacraments, the Christian life and so on. Here are two examples.

Article VII. Of the Lord Jesus Christ.

We believe in and confess the Lord Jesus Christ, the only Mediator between God and man, who, being the Eternal Son of God, for us men and for our salvation became truly man, being conceived of the Holy Spirit and born of the Virgin Mary, yet without sin. Unto us He has revealed the Father, by His word and Spirit, making known the perfect will of God. For our redemption, He fulfilled all righteousness, offered Himself a perfect sacrifice on the Cross, satisfied Divine justice, and made propitiation for the sins of the whole world. He rose from the dead and ascended into Heaven, where He ever intercedes for us. In the hearts of believers He abides forever as the indwelling Christ; above us and over us all He rules; wherefore, unto Him we render love, obedience, and adoration as our Prophet, Priest, and King.

Article XIX. Of the Resurrection, the Last Judgment, and the Future Life.

We believe that there shall be a resurrection of the dead, both of the just and of the unjust, through the power of the Son of God, who shall come to judge the living and the dead; that the finally impenitent shall go away into eternal punishment and the righteous into life eternal.

When I was ordained, I was asked if I was in agreement with the 20 Articles of Faith. I was. Today, candidates for ministry in the United Church who are about to be ordained are asked if they are in "essential" agreement with those credal statements. I suspect most of them have their fingers thoroughly crossed behind their backs as they reply as, I suspect, do many people in the pews. The word essential opens the door to the broadest of interpretations. In the vernacular, "Yeah, sort of."

Since 1977, the year I was ordained, the United Church has created newer statements of faith to reflect changes in thinking and speaking, but it was time in my journey to take another look at some of the basic tenets of orthodox Christian faith. Did I still believe them? Where to begin?

The first two chapters of the New Testament contain five claims to fulfilled prophecy. The first of those was that Jesus would be born of a virgin. The doctrine of the virgin birth seemed like a logical place to start.

Matthew quotes Isaiah in his first attempt to establish the divinity of Jesus. What Isaiah wrote was, "Therefore the Lord himself will give you a sign: Behold, a virgin will be with child and bear a son, and she will call His name Immanuel" (Isaiah 7:14). Both Matthew and Luke were eager to make the life of Jesus conform to Old Testament prophecy so they insisted that Mary conceived as a virgin.

There are two problems here. The first is that the quote is taken completely out of context. Isaiah's verse is about a civil war between Israel and Judah. Ahaz, the king of Judah, is afraid of a new attack by the kings of Syria and Israel, who have just failed to take Jerusalem. Isaiah the prophet was saying that the baby would be a "sign" that the siege of Jerusalem would fail. In short, it was a local prophecy.

The other problem is that the Hebrew original does not use the word "virgin" (bethulah) but the word for "young woman" (haalmah); that is, a woman of childbearing age who had not yet given birth and who might or might not be a virgin. Matthew translates Isaiah 7:14 using the Greek word "parthenos" which means "virgin". What we have here is a mistranslation in the sense that it alters the meaning of Isaiah's original Hebrew. As I noted earlier, the gospel writers were not writing historical narratives, but writing to convince the reader of a truth they held. Matthew seemed more intent on making a statement about Jesus than doing good scholarship.

The other two gospels, Mark and John, don't seem to know about the virgin birth. Paul writes that Jesus is born of Joseph and Mary. He refers to Jesus as "born of the seed of David according to the flesh" (Romans 1:3) and "born of woman" (Galatians 4:4), inferring that Jesus was a human with no reference to his mother's virginity. So the maniacal insistence by some that Jesus had to be virgin-born is rooted, among other reasons, in a mistranslation from Hebrew.

What about the doctrine of original sin and the requisite atoning sacrifice of Jesus on the cross? The crucifixion is considered necessary because all humans are born in sin. All little babies, before they have had a thought or done anything, are riddled with sin. St. Thomas Aquinas wrote "... the original sin of all men was in Adam indeed, as in its principal cause, according to the words of the Apostle (Romans 5:12): 'In whom all have sinned': whereas it is in the bodily semen, as in its instrumental cause, since it is by the active power of the semen that original sin together with human nature is transmitted to the child." [25]

So Adam bequeathed his "sin" in his bodily semen, the first sexually transmitted disease it would seem, to the entire human race. This sin with which all newborns are stained was apparently so terrible that it could be forgiven only through the blood sacrifice of a scapegoat. If the creator of everything was inclined to forgive us, why didn't he just forgive us? In the Lord's Prayer, we humans are encouraged to forgive those who have sinned against us without asking for a payment. Why did God need the shedding of blood in order to forgive?

Expiation by animal sacrifice is ancient and pervasive. We've all heard of the scapegoat, an innocent sacrificed to appease an angry deity. If you've taken the brief voyage on the Niagara Falls boat called the Maid of the Mist, you may know where the boat's name comes from. When the people of a nearby

First Nation's village began to get sick and die, they felt they must please the thunder god Hinum, who lived in the falls. They began by sacrificing food items, sending them over the falls in a canoe. That didn't work. So they put the daughter of the chief in a canoe and sent her over the falls. Alas, the most beautiful maiden of the tribe lost her life to appease the thunder god. The maid of the mist.

Christianity maintains that even though the chief priests would send a goat into the wilderness to die after they had symbolically laid the sins of the people on it (according to Leviticus 16), the stain of sin was so great that no ordinary scapegoat would suffice to cleanse the human race. The only adequate victim was God himself. So the crucifixion of the divine Christ was a fully sufficient offering of blood to a deity who requires it to expiate the sin of Adam (Hebrews 9:22-28). In this case, God is both judge and victim, if you accept the notion of the Trinity.

Few people believe Adam ever existed except as a symbol of the separation of humanity from its creator. So I questioned how, if Adam never existed, the disease of sin could be passed down from him, human to human. As Richard Dawkins puts it in characteristic bluntness, "Jesus had himself tortured and executed, in vicarious punishment for a symbolic sin committed by a non-existent individual."[26] Needless to say, the doctrine of original sin and the work of the cross seemed more and more to me like the dirt created by the vacuum salesman who just happens to have the means to deal with it.

Linked to the doctrine of sin and the cross is the teaching on the sacrament of Holy Communion or Eucharist, in which the sacrifice of Jesus is regularly revisited. There are different ideas of what's happening here. Protestants hold the notion of consubstantiation, meaning the bread and wine are symbolic and you eat and drink the body and blood of Jesus with ("con" is Latin for "with") the bread and wine. The Roman Catholic Church holds to a notion of transubstantiation, that the wine and wafer are mysteriously transformed into the body and blood of Jesus. Not symbolically or allegorically, mind you, but really transformed! All over the world, at the moment a priest elevates the baker's bread and the vintner's nectar, the flesh and blood of a resurrected first-century Jew reappears in its eternal freshness, unchanged. According to the 16th-century Council of Trent "... there is a change of the whole substance of

the bread into the body, and of the whole substance of the wine into blood."
With all respect to my Roman Catholic friends, it's more inconceivable than
a rabbit being pulled out of an empty hat.

But here's the thing. If you don't believe that that's what's happening at the
communion table, then you can't participate. That is why Protestants are not
welcome to partake in the Eucharist at Catholic mass. I used to get quite
indignant whenever a priest would invite me along with all other non-Catholics
to come forward and fold my hands and ask for a blessing instead of the bread.
I'd fume and sit on my hands in the pew instead. But at this point in my life,
the squabble over what is or is not happening at communion seems as relevant
and as fruitful as arguing over the correct order of Santa's reindeer, behind
Rudolph of course.

Such debates make the issues and assertions of Christianity appear totally
unrelated to the life experiences of the person in the pew. As Ralph Waldo
Emerson said in his address to the senior class in Divinity College Cambridge
in 1838, "I once heard a preacher who sorely tempted me to say I would go
to church no more. A snowstorm was falling around us. The snow-storm was
real, the preacher merely spectral, and the eye felt the sad contrast in looking
at him, and then out of the window behind him into the beautiful meteor
of the snow."[27]

The death of Jesus was temporary, of course. Three days later he rose from the
dead. What are we to make of the story of the resurrection? To return briefly
to biblical scholarship, we only have hearsay evidence of the resurrection at
best. No one said, "I was there when Jesus rose from the grave." As John Loftus
points out, "We have no independent reports that the veil of the temple was
torn in two at Jesus' death (Mark 15:38), or that darkness came 'over the whole
land' from noon until three in the afternoon (Mark 15:33), or that 'the sun
stopped shining' (Luke 23:45) or that there was an earthquake at his death
(Matt. 28:2) or that the saints were raised to life at his death and 'went into
the holy city and appeared to many people' and were never heard from again
(Matt. 27:52-53)".[28] No Roman or rabbinic literature mentions them. Stories
of the resurrection of Jesus come from those who were not there.

Adding to the hearsay of the reports is that rumours of magic were rampant
in those days. It was easy to believe in miraculous tales. Jesus wasn't the first

person to come alive post-mortem. The list of dying and rising gods is long. One prototype for Jesus' resurrection is found in the central myth of ancient Egypt of Osiris and Isis. Osiris was divine but lived on Earth, suffered betrayal and death and after mutilation, he rose again. He was so exalted that he became the equal and sometimes even the superior of Ra, the sun god. Osiris and his sister Isis had a son Horus. Both Osiris and Horus were "the god-human, the being who was both divine and human," according to Sir Wallis Budge, the keeper of Egyptian and Assyrian antiquities in the British Museum. I don't have to hammer home the obvious parallels with Christian theology, just to point out that Jesus wasn't the first to have allegedly risen from the grave.

The resurrection of Jesus is, as it always has been, an article of faith that lies at the very core of Christianity. As St. Paul wrote, "If Christ has not been raised, your faith is worthless" (1 Corinthians 15:17).

The list of Christian doctrines is long, including who God is, who Christ is, what heaven is like and how you get there. But now you know why my fingers were tightly crossed for some time before I retired from full-time ministry.

Since then, while volumes of opinion continue to flow from doctrinal debates and divisions, I am resigned not to waste precious time in this life to argue over the difference between, say, the *substance* and *essence* of the body and blood of Christ at the Eucharist (the bread and wine appear to look the same but their substance has changed) and whatever modern equivalents we have of Thomas Aquinas' discussion of questions regarding angels such as, "Can several angels be in the same place?"[29]

I am content in the knowledge that those who wrote and edited the scriptures lived in an era far different from ours. They were not intellectually inferior, but in the absence of knowledge of the natural world to which we are privy, they were open to fantastic tales told by those with either perceived authority or honest sincerity.

Theirs indeed was a strange world where a snake and a donkey could talk, where people could live more than 900 years, where a woman could be turned into a pillar of salt and the sun would be halted in its course across the sky, a world where a star could lead three men to a stable, where people could instantly start to speak a foreign tongue and a man could be swallowed by a whale, and live. It was a world where someone could walk on the water, demons made people sick and someone's shadow could heal people.

We still harbour strange superstitions. Hotel elevators "skip" the 13th floor. People still read their horoscopes in the morning newspaper. When I travelled in northern Thailand, I passed tiny spirit houses, not unlike our bird houses, where locals would place some fruit to appease the spirits so there would be less sickness. Of course we know what causes sickness today, just as we know why it rains. But in the absence of knowing about germs and viruses today, as well as in biblical times, superstition remains rampant and there is a naive gullibility that some find comedic.

Today if someone walked into a bar and told everyone their ass talked, you can imagine the reaction. But someone believed Balaam's story and it made its way into the Old Testament (Numbers 22:21-39). Now imagine that you read a story about someone's ass talking and it came from, say, Hindu scripture. Would you reject it as man-made mythology because you were born in North America and raised in a Christian home? Would you accept it if you were born in India? How do we tell the difference between a divine miracle and a crazy story? I was coming to realize that I accepted miraculous biblical stories as truth and wrote off other religions as legends because of my conversion, rather than any assessment of their plausibility. I also could no longer avoid asking why donkeys don't talk today. And why aren't the dead raised anymore? Is the age of miracles over or do we simply accept stories because they are tucked neatly into the ancient past?

Maladies such as epilepsy or psychiatric disabilities were once considered symptoms of demon possession. It is not unreasonable to say that our understanding of maladies has changed. What were once considered spiritual afflictions are now understood as chemical imbalances in the brain.

While we still have our quirky superstitions, we are for the most part skeptical of claims that defy reason, such as casting out demons and giving sight to the blind. In the New Testament, Jesus made a little magic mud with his saliva and dirt and put it on a blind man's eyes. When the man washed his eyes, he could see (John 9:1-7). Jesus also gave permission for a host of demons named Legion to leave a man and enter a herd of pigs which promptly proceeded to stampede over a cliff and drown themselves in the sea (Mark 5:6-13).

Yes, I know the rebuttal that God can do anything and that sometimes we just have to accept things on faith. It's just that I was having a harder and harder time believing stories that emerged from an era rife with miraculous tales, in the absence of our understanding of the world around us and within us.

I mention superstition under the rubric of dogma because believers are too ready to accept on faith, without a shred of evidence, completely irrational tales and teachings some would call superstitions. Under any other circumstances, certain articles of faith would be rejected outrightly as absolutely incredulous: virgin birth, incarnation, substitutionary atonement, resurrection, transubstantiation.

How did all these strange notions come to be? As we know, Christianity was not born overnight, but evolved gradually over centuries through rigorous and sometimes nasty conflicts over competing doctrines. Philosopher and scientist Daniel Dennett suggests religion is natural and evolves through "intelligent" design and market forces[30]. Those market forces are not only competing, but are arbitrarily adopted. Just as believers cherry-pick the nice Bible verses, or at least the ones they can live with, so do they cherry-pick the doctrines they can live with. Just as many Roman Catholic women use contraception against the teaching of their Church, many believers discard doctrines they don't like and cross their fingers as they profess the rest.

While nit-picking over doctrine rightly seems petty in the grand scheme of things, my thoughts began to move toward the much larger and far grander question of how we got here in the first place.

---

[25] *Summa Theologica*: Question 83, Article 1, Objection 5

[26] Richard Dawkins, *The God Delusion*, 1st Mariner Books ed. (Boston: Houghton Mifflin Co., 2008). 287

[27] Ralph Waldo Emerson, Carl Bode, and Malcolm Cowley, *The Portable Emerson*, Rev. ed., The Viking Portable Library (New York: Penguin, 1981), 83.

[28] John W. Loftus, *Why I Became an Atheist : A Former Preacher Rejects Christianity*, Rev. and expanded ed. (Amherst, N.Y.: Prometheus Books, 2012), 412.

[29] *Summa Theologica* ca. 1270

[30] Daniel Clement Dennett, *Breaking the Spell : Religion as a Natural Phenomenon* (New York: Viking, 2006), 43.

CHAPTER NINE

· FROM THE BIG BANG TO DNA ·

Science flies us to the moon. Religion flies us into buildings.
Richard Dawkins

God is an ever-receding pocket of scientific ignorance.
Neil DeGrasse Tyson

God was invented to explain mystery.
Richard Feynman

Around the time I was revisiting the Bible, church history and doctrine, my wife and I were on a fishing trip in Alaska with friends from Canada's Yukon Territory. I remember the moment when, standing on the deck of their fishing trawler Madera, gazing at the barren beautiful snow-capped mountains with glaciers meandering down the side, I was overcome with awe and wonder.

What I realized in that moment, however, was that my awe was directed more at what I was looking at than a creator who was supposed to have made the mountain.

How did everything come to be? How did we come to be? These questions would form another signpost in my sojourn. I started to explore cosmology and biology. I was inspired and enthralled by the antiquity of the Earth and the antiquity of life. As I began to read books by biologist Richard Dawkins, I was captivated by the elegance and simplicity of Charles Darwin's theory of evolution by natural design; the notion that the history of our species is evolutionary and all living creatures are cousins with the same genetic code. I saw how change from genetic mutation and natural selection is imperceptibly gradual, of course, but that the evidence is unmistakable. I saw how evolution provided a powerful tool for both explaining the imperfections of species and accounting for transitional species. Facts are stubborn things and facts were getting in the way of me continuing to believe in the pleasant biblical stories of creation.

As an early 60th birthday gift, my three children pooled their resources and gave me a kit to participate in the Genographic Project, a partnership between the National Geographic Society and IBM with support from the Waitt Family Foundation. This five-year project hopes to build a large database of genetic information, using laboratory and computer analysis of DNA contributed by thousands of people around the world, to map the migratory history of the human species.

The DNA (deoxyribonucleic acid) molecule in the nuclei of our cells tells the story of who we are and where we came from. DNA's string of four chemical bases is shaped like a double-stranded helix or a twisted ladder you've likely seen. While 99.9 per cent of everyone's DNA is identical, geneticists study the tiny fraction that defines differences among us.

DNA is a document we can read almost like a history book. Y chromosomal DNA is passed from father to son. Mitochondrial DNA is passed from mother to child (both male and female). Y chromosome data has determined that the common ancestor of every man alive was an African, dubbed "Scientific Adam", who lived around 60,000 years ago. There is similar evidence of a common African origin for mitochondrial DNA or "Scientific Eve." This Adam and Eve were not a couple who necessarily lived at the same time but are our earliest traceable common ancestors. By following the genetic signature of the descendants of this "Adam and Eve," we can trace the human journey around the globe.

How? Our DNA is a combination of genes passed from both our mother and father, giving us traits from eye colour and height to athleticism and disease susceptibility. One exception is the Y chromosome, which is passed directly from father to son, unchanged, from generation to generation. Unchanged that is, unless a mutation, a random, naturally occurring, usually harmless change, occurs. The mutation, known as a marker, acts as an evolutionary signpost that defines different human lineages. Markers, which never disappear, allow the different branches of the human family tree to be traced back to their origin.

This way, genetic archeologists can pinpoint both the age and geographic origin of the most recent common ancestor of everyone alive who carries that marker.

The descendants of a small group of Africans multiplied over time and split into groups defined by their genetic markers and migrated across our planet. Y chromosome Adam and mitochondrial Eve were not the only two humans alive at the time and, again, they might not have actually been alive at the same time. But they were the luckiest since their genetic lineages are the only ones that did not die out over time.

The results from my DNA markers showed that my ancestors came (from most recent to oldest) from England and Europe by way of Central Asia, the Middle East and, eventually, Africa, about 50,000 years ago. The Genographic Project is not only closing the gaps of what we know about the ancestral map of humankind, it is verifying in fact a truth that we often bandy about inside and outside religious circles—that we are one human family. And by the way, you and I are both Africans.

At the same time I was studying rudimentary biology, I was also learning about cosmology, which suggests that the universe which is almost 14 billion years old, is made up of billions of galaxies and that our own galaxy, the Milky Way, contains between 200 and 400 billion stars and is so huge that even at the speed of light, it would take 100,000 years to travel across it. According to Richard Dawkins, we don't know how many planets there are in the vastness of astrological space, but a good estimate is 10 to the 20th power or 100 billion billion. That's a lot of planets.

Frankly, I was blown away by what we are discovering about the universe. Still am. How did this body of information square with my former belief in a deity who made it all and held it all and knew it all and would one day end it all? In my gut, it made such a belief seem rather juvenile. The age of the universe. The size of the universe. Our planet's place in that universe. In Carl Sagan's *Pale Blue Dot*, he writes, "How is it that hardly any major religion has looked at science and concluded, 'This is better than we thought! The Universe is much bigger than our prophets said, grander, more subtle, more elegant.'?"[31]

Perhaps because of my growing skepticism about the tenets of Christianity, and also perhaps because of my growing cynicism toward its history, I was growing seriously averse to the arrogance of the very idea that this grand universe was made with me in mind, that the Creator had a plan for my life from the very beginning, billions of years ago. At the same time, looking back, I understood where such a notion would find a receptive heart.

For some reason, we humans have a strong desire to believe the creation story to be true. I get that. After all, creationism affords our lives meaning and purpose and offers reassurance that what we do matters within some great scheme. When William Jennings Bryan took on evolution in a courtroom in Tennessee in 1925 in the famous Scopes "monkey trial", he acknowledged that he did not fully understand evolution but said that he fully understood its dangers; how it threatened to leave students feeling lost in a cold, impersonal universe. Given a choice, Bryan said, "I would rather begin with God and reason down than begin with a piece of dirt and reason up."[32]

Creationism, however, has its intellectual challenges. About 120 million citizens of the United States put the timing of the creation of the universe about 2500 years after the Babylonians and Sumerians learned to brew beer. Former U.S. president George Bush said about evolution that "the jury is still out." I guess he never went to a museum of natural history or even took a look around his Crawford Ranch at rock formations. It seems so hard for so many to embrace human evolution and, to borrow from Darwin's phrase in the closing sentence of *On the Origin of Species*, to find "grandeur in this view of life."[33]

Why had I never thought about cosmology and biology before my deconversion? I confess that I'm wired for the arts. My high school marks don't lie. I've always had a penchant for humanities over science. My passion, if you will, has been the human condition. Language and literature; theology and theatre. Still is.

But science has caught my attention. I'm not sure how this happened, or exactly when. Maybe it was seeing the breathtaking images of stars being born in distant galaxies courtesy of the Hubble Telescope or maybe it was going to Antarctica the month after my retirement from ministry to discover that fossils of Jurassic Age subtropical vegetation are buried there. The reason we find traces of vegetation in Antarctica is that the land wasn't always so close to the frozen South Pole but rested in more temperate climes. The continents have drifted over millions of years, at about the speed your fingernail grows.

At any rate, this deconverted soul now finds science absolutely fascinating.

The Latin origin for the word science, scientia, means "knowledge", but the word today denotes not just all knowledge but a range of knowledge and the enquiries that search for it; knowledge of the physical world through the enquires of biology, geology, meteorology, chemistry and physics as well as the interconnections of, say, biochemistry and astrophysics.

Scientists already know this but perhaps it feels so new to me because I've spent my entire adult life puzzling and promoting stories that attempt to explain the unexplainable. How did we get here? Why do bad things happen? What are the sun, moon and stars? Are we alone? All cultures have mythical explanations, from the polytheisms of Greece, Rome and Scandinavia, say, to the monotheisms of Judaism and its offshoots of Christianity and Islam.

So who really was the first person? We've read about Adam and Eve in a Garden of Eden. There's also the chief god of the Norse peoples, Odin, who is sometimes called Wotan or Woden, from which we get our "Wednesday." "Thursday" comes from another Norse god, Thor, but I digress. Odin was walking along the shore one day and found two tree trunks. One he turned into the first man, Ask. The other he turned into the first woman, Embla. The Egyptians explained night by thinking that the goddess Nut swallowed the sun. The Japanese once explained earthquakes by conjuring a gigantic catfish that carried the world on its back and created earthquakes when it flipped its tail.

Stories are wonderful. They are told and altered and retold around the campfire—a great flood, a great escape or a great battle. Our tales are shaped to meet our needs and aspirations for saviours and such. They fill gaps in knowledge until science comes along and closes the gaps. But when it comes to tales that try to explain something we are having trouble understanding, we have to step back and ask ourselves if we believe the story or the lesson of the story. And if it's just the lesson, then what really happened?

Which brings me back to science. Advances in the last half-century have unlocked secrets to our planet and cosmos that have puzzled our species since its genesis. We did not emerge in a garden or on a shore. What we know for sure is that the universe is expanding. Galaxies are hurtling away from one another embedded in an ever-stretching fabric of space and time. Asteroids, comets and planets are pirouetting in a cosmic ballet choreographed by the forces of gravity.

Our sun is one of the billions of stars that make up our galaxy but how many galaxies are there? We don't know. So far, astronomers have only been able to see about 10,000. the universe is very, very big. And we are very, very small.

What about us? Where did we come from? We are the products of a gradual process of natural selection. As Richard Dawkins points out, if you could somehow trace your lineage far enough, your 185-millionth-great-grandfather would turn out to be ... wait for it ... a fish.[34] Carl Sagan put our lineage wonderfully into perspective when he suggested that two billion years ago our ancestors were microbes; a half-billion years ago, fish; 100 million years ago, something like mice; 10 million years ago, arboreal apes; and a million years ago, proto-humans puzzling out the taming of fire. Our evolutionary lineage is marked by mastery of change. In our time, the pace is quickening.[35]

The Bible suggests that our bodies are fearfully and wonderfully made (Psalm 139:14), the assumption being that we have been lovingly created. What we know, of course, is that we were not made out of dust during a creator's busy week from which he mysteriously had to rest for a day. Rather, our bodies are a marvellous culmination of millions of years of adaptation. Think of it. Right now your body is balancing a host of chemicals to keep you alive. You are not aware of it and you are not in control of it. Your body just does it for you. There are multiple processes at work inside us all the time of which we are totally ignorant. For instance, there is more bacteria living and working in one centimetre of my colon than the number of people who have ever existed in the world. Makes you wonder what or who is in charge of our life?

Does science have all the answers? No. But science, from the perspective of this new enthusiast, thrives on what it can't explain. Science knows it doesn't know everything. If it did, it would stop. Whereas religion creates a mystery and is content to leave it there, science probes a mystery to disclose an explanation. This critical spirit, which is imbedded in scientific inquiry, I find to be wonderfully liberating. One of the most influential philosophers of the 20th century, Karl Popper, came up with the falsifiability thesis or the notion that what defines a scientific idea is that it can be falsified. In his view, the work of scientists is not to look for evidence that their theories are correct, but to look for evidence that their theories are false. I'm drawn to the approach of science that is exploratory, testable and always revisable in the light of new or better evidence. When religion is confronted with contrary evidence, it attacks the messenger and digs in its heels a little deeper. As it has been said of preachers, when they don't know what they're talking about, they yell a little louder and pound the pulpit harder. Often it feels as if the tactic is adopted on a much larger scale by the more bombastic people of faith.

Does science solve all our personal problems such as fear, loneliness, sadness or anger? Not at all. That, I'm afraid, is up to us. These days, however, I get goosebumps with the changing seasons, knowing why they change. I am awed by the immensity of the night sky, knowing more about what I'm seeing than just twinkling stars. I am breathless with the realization that considering all the species of life that have evolved and perished on this planet, I am alive right here and right now. I'll admit that when I gaze at the night sky, I feel so inspired and at the same time so small. There is so much we don't know and what we don't know can be overwhelming. There are many questions about the origin of the universe and the place of our pale blue dot (to borrow from Carl Sagan).[36]

Where does it all come from? How did life get its start? I once was in awe of the wonder and majesty of a deity who was alleged to have made everything and who knew all of my thoughts. Today my awe has not diminished one iota but it springs from a new source based on what we know and what we don't know about everything. So I listen to podcasts about black holes and galaxies.

No matter what you currently believe, thinking outside the box of belief should not be considered irreverent. Is there any reason why what we believe cannot be tested by thoughtful evidence from outside the realm of religious orthodoxy? Sadly, the legacy of Christianity thinking outside the box is not good. The early Church seemed to set the tone when there was a great burning of books. The writer of Acts goes to the trouble of calculating the market value of the torched tomes, pointing out the sum as if it were a monetary victory over incorrect thinking (Acts 19:19).

Emperor Constantine took up the torch, so to speak, when he sent philosophers into exile, declaring them social outcasts. The Inquisition and the creation of the *Index of Forbidden Books* epitomized the campaign to eradicate all opinion that deviated from the doctrine of the Roman Church. For the record, the final (20th) edition appeared in 1948 and it was only formally abolished on June 14, 1966 by Pope Paul VI.

In the spirit of the book of Genesis and the original sin of Adam eating the fruit of knowledge, understanding has been tainted as ungodly; its only service is to distance us from God. The Church was convinced, then, that the Bible contains all the knowledge one needs, or all the Church needs I suppose. The church, sadly, has a record of handling new discoveries by persecuting the discoverer.

Why? Has the Church been fearful that new information might contradict what it has deemed to be reality? In the fourth century, St. Augustine wrote, "Besides this there is yet another form of temptation still more complex in its peril. For in addition to the fleshly appetite which strives for the gratification of all senses and pleasures—in which its slaves perish because they separate themselves from thee—there is also a certain vain and curious longing in the soul, rooted in the same bodily senses, which is cloaked under the name of knowledge and learning; not having pleasure in the flesh, but striving for new experiences through the flesh. This longing—since its origin is our appetite for learning, and since the sight is the chief of our senses in the acquisition of knowledge—is called in the divine language 'the lust of the eyes.'" (Confessions Chapter 35:54)

Galileo Galilei is probably the poster child of Christianity's hostility toward knowledge and science. The issue at the time was heliocentrism. While Italian Renaissance painters looked at people and saw angels, Galileo looked at the heavens and didn't see angels. The Pope and the Inquisition condemned Galileo because he argued that the Earth was a satellite of a sun located at the centre of a solar system.

For centuries it was forbidden to read the Bible without the mediation of priests. People could not be trusted with the written word lest they apply reason, analysis and criticism along with the findings of the historians and geologists. But if God has given us a mind, why should we be prohibited from using it to investigate, experiment and possibly understand?

Too many of us have life by the tail and are not about to reveal a lack of knowledge by asking a question or submitting to authority. The more questions I was asking about the fundamentals of my faith, the more I realized that some people of faith don't even like questions. They are averse to curiosity, as if asking a hard question is somehow an insult to a God they trust. Orthodoxy is their sanctuary from the evidence of science. God said it. I believe it. That settles it. They don the straitjacket of correct believing to feel safe. They dutifully recite a creedal statement but are averse to entertaining questions about what it is they really believe. As George Meredith wrote in his poem *Modern Love*, "Ah, what a dusty answer gets the soul/When hot for certainties in this our life." [37]

Why is faith not receptive to satire? Is it a symptom of a lack of self-confidence or unquestioning iron conviction or both? Rather than being enshrined, doctrines and creeds should be hung on question marks. We ought to be intellectually honest enough to admit that when it comes to life and faith, questions outnumber answers.

And questions are not to be merely tolerated. They are to be honoured. If what I believe is true, it can surely stand up to my questions. If it isn't true, then it deserves to be shaken and stirred. I'm not a scientist. Never will be. But at this point in my life, it seems more fascinating and fruitful to learn about what we actually know and what we are exploring than to argue over which supernatural explanation for life and its woes is the correct one.

---

[31] Carl Sagan, *Pale Blue Dot : A Vision of the Human Future in Space*, 1st ed. (New York: Random House, 1994). 50

[32] http://law2.umkc.edu/faculty/projects/ftrials/conlaw/bryanwilliam.html

[33] Charles Darwin, *On the Origin of Species*, 1859, The Works of Charles Darwin (Washington Square, N.Y.: New York University Press, 1988). 540

[34] Richard Dawkins and Dave McKean, *The Magic of Reality : How We Know What's Really True*, 1st Free Press hardcover ed. (New York: Free Press, 2011), 39-40.

[35] Carl Sagan, *Pale Blue Dot : A Vision of the Human Future in Space*, 1st ed. (New York: Random House, 1994), 332.

[36] Ibid.

[37] George Meredith, *Modern Love, and Other Poems*, Old World Series 12 (Portland, Me.,: T. B. Mosher, 1898). 3

CHAPTER TEN

· THE END ·

Most people cannot bear sitting in church for an hour on a Sunday.
How are they supposed to live somewhere very similar to it for an eternity?
Mark Twain

That vast, moth-eaten musical brocade
Created to pretend we never die.
Phllip Larkin (Aubade)

No serious study of religious faith would be complete without a peek into what allegedly lies ahead for the believer. As a dear friend and colleague in ministry always says to me, "life is good, you die, and then it gets better". (It depends on what you believe, of course, but we'll come to that.)

There are two ends in mind here. One is our personal end, as the date of our demise draws inexorably closer with every passing day. The other is the notion of an apocalyptic end of time itself. Let's start with our personal death and the popular notion of heaven.

Almost everyone who stands sadly in front of the casket of a friend has wondered if this life is all there is. Do we go out like a match or does our light shine as we go on burning somewhere else? When we shed our corporeal ballast, do we sail away to a paradise with all the qualities and amenities of a Caribbean cruise?

We have always fought our inevitable demise and given ourselves answers wrapped in fables and fairy tales. We've tried to ward off death by eliminating it in our minds. Belief in life after life has been a powerful antidote to the terror many feel at the very thought of death as extinction. It has also been a source of great comfort in the face of losing a loved one, hoping and anticipating that day when we will be reunited with them in a future time and place. Faced with the cold reality that virtue isn't always rewarded in this life, religion has also offered the notion of posthumous reward in another life for virtue in this one.

Like most Christians, I was convinced that I was immortal. I had accepted Jesus as my Lord and Saviour. I just knew that when the heart that beats strong in my chest stops beating, which it inevitably will, I would experience something like falling asleep in one room and waking up in another, a room that Jesus had prepared for me, as He promised. After He had shared the Passover meal with His disciples and was on his way to his death, He is quoted as saying, *"Do not let your hearts be troubled. Believe in God. Believe also in me. In my Father's house there are many rooms. I go to prepare a place for you and will come again and take you to myself, that where I am, you may be also"* (John 14:3).

Descriptions of the details of this new room were mostly formed by the lyrics of hymns. Any tears of sadness will be wiped away. There will be great joy that just goes on and on. And, of course, there will be lots and lots of praising. *When we've been there 10,000 years, bright shining as the sun, we've no less days to sing God's praise than when we've first begun.* At least that's what we sing in John Newton's song *Amazing Grace*.

There are many other gospel chestnuts anticipating this glorious place such as *When the Roll is Called Up Yonder, Mansion on a Hill, I'll Fly Away, Blessed Assurance.* The list goes on and on. With such a magnificent promise, how can you be a Christian and not look forward to dying?

The notion that we somehow survive death is the hallmark of most religious belief. Post-mortem pie in the sky is the delicious hope of every Christian. St. Paul said that life for him was Christ and so, naturally, to die would be gain because he'd be with his Lord. While Paul was heavenly minded, he also wanted to hang around in order to do some earthly good. Looking back over the years of ministering to many who were dying, most rational sick people and their relatives want every medical intervention possible to prolong life, even if they do subscribe to a promise of paradise after death. I understood that. It's great to be alive in this life and at the same time, it will be great to be alive forever.

I've long lost count of how many funerals I have conducted. But every time it was my privilege to lead a service for the burial of the dead, I began with the words recorded in the gospel of John, in which Jesus brings comfort to a woman (Martha) who has lost her brother (Lazarus) whom Jesus loved and would soon bring back to life. *"I am the resurrection and the life; he who believes in Me shall live even if he died, and everyone who lives and believes in Me shall never die"* (John 11:26).

I always felt comfort in those words and hoped that mourners would also take comfort in them. It was jarring for me to hear those who didn't believe in life after life. The late John Lennon invited us to imagine there's no heaven. How could you do that? Why would you do that? Heaven forbid!

Then along came cosmologist Stephen Hawking, who said that not only does he not imagine there's a heaven, he believes there's no heaven. The 69-year-old who was expected to die at age 21 after being diagnosed with degenerative motor neuron disease but went on to become one the world's renowned scientists, suggests that an eternal realm where we'll strum harps and intone hallelujahs "is a fairy story for people afraid of the dark."

But Jesus told his disciples he was going to get a place ready for them, and the hope of going to that place and seeing others there has been comfort to his followers ever since. How could anyone begrudge someone else such comfort? When musician Eric Clapton lost his four-year-old son Conor in 1991, he co-wrote in the song *Tears in Heaven,*

Would you hold my hand if I saw you in heaven?

Would you help me stand if I saw you in heaven?

Beyond the door there's peace I'm sure,

And I know there'll be no more tears in heaven.

We talk with great assurance about life after life. Some offer "proofs" in the form of near-death experiences. There are always fresh testimonies of those whose experiences have been interpreted as an indication, and to some clear evidence, that we survive our demise. There is a typical pattern. Someone who is either dying or temporarily clinically dead passes through a tunnel toward a light. Often there is someone who meets them. Interestingly, people of different traditions interpret the being according to their tradition. Christians meet Jesus. First Nations folk meet the Great Spirit. Chinese people meet an ancestor.

Psychologist and science historian Michael Shermer has attempted to explain that belief in an afterlife as an extension of our brain's normal ability to imagine ourselves somewhere else in both space and time.[38] We are natural-born immortalists. People of faith may come up with rational reasons for believing in an afterlife, but the belief always comes first and the reasons follow.

Despite the assurances of faith and the occasional near-death experience, a down-to-earth look at heaven reveals that it, not to mention the concomitant destination of hell, is an imprecise place. Where is it? How do you get there? Who goes there? Who will we meet? Will there be any surprises? I used to joke that the two most common queries in heaven will be, "Where's so-and-so?" and "What are you doing here?"

This second question raises some unsettling ideas about the prospect of living forever with family and fellow Christians. In moments of candour, some wince at the prospect of eternity with certain church people and relish the bonhomie of gregarious, albeit imperfect, sinners. In the maxim attributed to Mark Twain, "heaven for the climate, hell for the company."[39]

Hawking's notion of heaven as a fairy tale is rooted in a scientific worldview in which there is nothing beyond the moment when the brain flickers for the last time. Lennon's invitation to imagine no heaven, however, was rooted in the notion that the conflicting ideas of who gets to heaven and what gets you there, divides rather than unites; destroys rather than creates.

I was starting to realize that Lennon (not my favourite Beatle, mind you) was making a good point. Believing in heaven is not benign. There are strong disagreements among believers over who is going to get there.

There was a time when I used to laugh at how certain Christian denominations are convinced that THEY are the ones going to heaven and the rest of the alleged believers most definitely are not. I don't laugh anymore. Heaven has become a serious, deadly idea. As we know, the anticipation of divine reward has moved people to commit acts of monstrous evil. With macabre mirth, we still snicker at the bizarre image of the 9/11 hijackers luxuriating in carnal delights with virgins in return for their mass murder of thousands of innocent souls.

Even accumulating good deeds as bargaining chips for eternal bliss is a troublesome morality that reduces God to Santa Claus, who knows if you've been bad or good, so be good for goodness sake.

Imagine no heaven? Really? Imagine Manhattan's Twin Towers still standing. Imagine no beheading of blasphemers. Imagine no Inquisition. It's not easy. But for Lennon, Hawking et al, it's worth a try.

Believing in an afterlife offers comfort in the face of death. I've heard it expressed so often in the comments of mourners that their beloved had gone to a better place to be reunited with family. They take comfort in the notion that others have gone ahead of us to the place where, God willing, we will join them and all the rest of the redeemed. Christians rhapsodize about walking through pearly gates on streets paved with gold while they play harps without taking lessons and sing a lot of choral alleluias. Once through the gates, we may see grandma and perhaps have a game of euchre with the old gang up there. We may also bump into the guy who was such a jerk to us on Earth but somehow it'll all be fine and won't it be good to finally get there? As the old gospel song goes, *"This world is not my home, I'm just a'passin through."*

Christianity offers one view of heaven. In Jewish apocalyptic literature, suffering of the righteous in this life is temporary since God will someday intervene and make everything okay. There will be a new kingdom of peace and justice where the wicked will be destroyed and the poor and oppressed will rule.

Passages from the Quran known as Hadith describe a post-mortem paradise of rivers, trees and cool breezes in blessed contrast to desert climes. Unlike a Christian heaven where, according to Jesus, there's no marriage and such, the Quran promises carnal delights. The virtuous are reclining either on thrones, green cushions or carpets attended by "companions" with "beautiful, big and lustrous eyes." These companions are promised as a reward to the faithful Muslim. Fair enough. But getting to heaven, as I mentioned earlier, is where things get confusing and even dangerous to the non-believer. Confusing because of how heaven is used and misused.

I'm ashamed to admit that religious leaders have used the next life as a fund-raising tool or a bludgeon to impose discipline on the faithful. Who can forget the late evangelist Oral Roberts saying that if donors didn't come through with $8 million, God was going to call him home? The only thing worse than the empty threat was that it worked! The money rolled in.

The very idea of eternity being a long, long time can be disquieting. A colleague in ministry used to say with refreshing candour that he would look forward to about 1000 years of heaven, but that would be it. Some of the faithful hope for heaven but get frustrated when there's nothing good on television. As Susan Ertz wrote in her novel *Anger in the Sky*, "Someone has somewhere commented on the fact that millions long for immortality who don't know what to do with themselves on a rainy Sunday afternoon."[40]

Certain aspirations of paradise are perilous even if you don't believe in heaven. Citizens of Canada, as well as the United States and Great Britain, are continually vigilant against al-Qaeda-inspired terrorist attacks. I finished the 2013 Boston Marathon a few minutes before the bombs went off, bombs set by young men who converted to Islam. It was a sound I never want to hear again.

As for the late 9/11 hijackers, suicide bombers in Spain and Britain and elsewhere, the only explanation for their self-immolation is that they actually believe that if they trade in their lives for the privilege of killing others, they will go straight to paradise for doing so. You don't want to be around when an Islamic jihadist wants to go to paradise.

So while a Christian may be motivated or driven to be good by the prospect of heaven, and a Jew longs for the kingdom where there is peace and justice, a Muslim may be motivated to martyrdom and murder by the same prospect of bliss.

You might think that those who have no hope in an afterlife must be miserable in this life. Let me assure you that is not the case. While I no longer believe in a place or state of bliss after death, every day of this life is heavenly, in the sense of being full of bliss. There's much to love and learn and if I can lengthen my days by running religiously and eating sensibly, so be it.

Yes, I must confess that in this journey I was initially troubled by the idea that my death brought my annihilation. But then I started to wonder what was so awful if, when we die, that's it? Finis. What if there's no heaven, as John Lennon suggested we imagine? What if when we are gone, we simply don't exist anymore? I thought long and hard about that notion. I asked myself, "Where was I a year before I was born?" I didn't exist. Period. A year before you were born, you didn't exist either. So it seems reasonable, albeit sad, that when I die, I will return to not existing. The state of being dead is the same as the state of being unborn. It's not a happy thought, I admit, but it's based on what seems real and not what I hope to be true. Religion seems to suggest that if we think we are immortal, then we are; that an exception to the rules of annihilation will be made in our case and we will escape the carnage of a Judgement due to those who don't believe. Thinking something doesn't always make it so.

But there's another way to look at it. The fact that I'm going to die is good news because it means that I lived; that I was lucky enough to have existed at all. Considering the randomness of life, that our planet is located in such a "sweet spot" in our solar system to sustain life, coupled with the fact that after billions of years of evolution, I'm the product of the coupling of two people who were the products of the coupling of four people and so on exponentially, it's amazing that I'm here at all. Life seems so precious to me these days. I love it and I want to go on as long as possible. I want to maintain a childlike wonder as long as I am able. As the Roman Emperor Marcus Auelius wrote, "it is not death that men should fear, rather he should fear never beginning to live."

I know that it may be unsettling to contemplate that we won't be united with our family or our pets or with Jesus in a spiritual realm forever. But what does it say about us if we are prepared to believe something because it brings us comfort even when we know in our heart and mind that it isn't true?

Beyond our personal end, there is the prospect of our collective demise with the apocalyptic end of time itself. It goes by different names: the Final Judgement; The End Times (or Eschaton); the Second Coming of Christ (or Parousia).

There was a time when I, like almost every follower of Jesus, including Jesus himself as recorded in Matthew 24:29-34, was confident that the end was imminent and God would break into history again very soon. Hal Lindsey's 1970 book, *The Late Great Planet Earth* compared end-time prophecies in the Bible with then-current events in an attempt to predict the rapture of believers before the thousand-year tribulation and the Second Coming of Christ. Lindsey originally suggested the possibility that these climactic events might play out in the 1980s. He cited an increase in the frequency of famines, wars and earthquakes as definitive signs of the times that the end of the world was near.

Of course Lindsey was off in his prediction. Frankly, so has everyone been who has ventured to pinpoint the return of Christ. Even in the Bible, we read of critics who were questioning why Jesus hadn't returned in the generation he said he would. The writer of the second epistle of Peter counters with a little heavenly mathematics that "with the Lord one day is as a thousand years ..." (2 Peter 3:8). Over the centuries Christians have gerrymandered biblical texts to come up with different estimates of the end of time, followed by reasons why the predictions were off. The game continues as new anti-Christs, new Babylons and new Jerusalems are created to substitute for the old ones.

When Christopher Columbus arrived in the Americas, landing in the Bahamas, he believed he had found the terrestrial paradise promised in the book of Revelation. Columbus wrote of his journey, "God made me the messenger of the new heaven and the new earth of which he spoke in the Apocalypse of St. John ... and he showed me the spot where to find it." [41]

The tradition in America of seeing events through the lens of end-time biblical prophesy of a world purified by catastrophe and then redeemed and made Christian with the return of Jesus continues unabated. Social scientist J. W. Nelson notes that apocalyptic ideas are as American as the hotdog. Television evangelist Dr. Jack Van Impe (he holds a whopping 15 doctorates), has made a lot of money feeding the hysteria of the apocalyptic mind by predicting the end times over and over again as the dates pass uneventfully.

The apocalyptic minds of Van Impe et al tend to demonize others with assurances that other faiths who are clearly worshipping false deities, along with those of no faith, will not be spared the fires of hell.

What happened to my belief in the imminent Second Coming of Christ? It likely went the way of my belief in Jesus as an invisible friend who monitored my thoughts, whom I now consider to be an apocryphal preacher. It was he who was sure God was about to intervene in history within his generation.

The belief in the return of Christ may also have been eroded by the very idea common among believers that when Jesus returns, there's going to be massive chaos and death. Tribulation is the catchword. Why would any deity, let alone a deity of love, justice and mercy, kill billions of people just because they were born at the wrong time in human history, into the wrong faith or were just too skeptical to believe? Why do Christians almost delight in the prospect that while those who are alive when Jesus returns will be caught up in the air to be with Jesus forever at the end of time, the rest of this poor human race will be left behind to suffer somehow?

I'm also nervous about fanatic Muslim, Jewish and Christian extremists who are pathologically motivated to hurry up the apocalypse. It is not too much of a stretch to imagine that conflict over the ownership of the Temple Mount in Jerusalem, for instance, could easily escalate into a nuclear confrontation. No matter what the death toll might be, some would welcome it as a sign of Christ's imminent return. If we allow carbon dioxide levels in the atmosphere to rise uncontrollably due to the impact of our species thinking that it is God's will, then we are all literally sunk.

Those who desperately wish to live to see as many days as possible, should be free to do so without having their lives shortened by someone's warped view of what their deity has in store for the future.

Why are some people so ready to welcome a catastrophic end of history? I understand that if we look at our species in the form of a narrative, with a creation myth as chapter one, we will naturally look for a final chapter to play out. I also understand that when life is inexplicably chaotic at the hands of others, we will naturally fantasize of imminent salvation for ourselves, supernatural retribution for our enemies and restoration of order in a new and perfect society.

What I cannot accept is the fatalism that accompanies a wish for the end of time. Consider the chilling words of Ayatollah Khomeini, quoted in an Iranian school textbook, "Either we shake one another's hands in joy at the victory of Islam in the world, or all of us will turn to eternal life and martyrdom. In both cases, victory and success are ours."

No matter what your religion, end times scenarios and their concomitant death-wish, whatever the details, seem so ethically distasteful, not to mention physically preposterous, that I'm no longer looking for signs of the times, getting caught up in the latest predictions of Christ's return. I'm looking at a future which is bright but for entirely different reasons.

[38] Michael Shermer, *The Believing Brain: From Ghosts and Gods to Politics and Conspiracies—How We Construct Beliefs and Reinforce Them as Truths,* 1st ed. (New York: Times Books, 2011), 144.

[39] The maxim is also attributed to J.M. Barrie sometime around 1890.

[40] Susan Ertz, *Anger in the Sky* (New York and London: Harper & Brothers, 1943). 137

[41] Balmer, Randall. *"Apocalypticism in American Culture."* Divining America, TeacherServe©. National Humanities Center.1.

CHAPTER ELEVEN
· BEYOND BELIEF ·

Atheism is a religion like not collecting stamps is a hobby.
Penn Jillette

There are moments when one has to choose between living one's own
life, fully, entirely, completely – or dragging out some false, shallow,
degrading existence that the world in its hypocrisy demands."
Oscar Wilde (Lady Windermere's Fan)

Speak what you think now in hard words and tomorrow speak
what to-morrow thinks in hard words again, though it contradict
every thing you said to-day – 'Ah, so you shall be sure to be
misunderstood.' – Is it so bad then to be misunderstood?
Ralph Waldo Emerson (Self-Reliance)

So where do we go from here? Where do I go from here? If I'm no longer a Christian, who am I? What's my label? Do I need a new label at all?

In one sense, labelling is natural and normal. Music labels identify the companies that have invested in the artists and paid to let them make their music and make the companies money. Manufacturers sew labels on shirts, shoes and purses to give marketing tips, cleaning instructions, buyers' bragging rights and general information: who made it, where it was made, what it's made from, genuine or imitation.

When it comes to labels for people, we like to have a pigeonhole in which to put them. We slap on an epithet, sometimes pejorative, to sum up the totality of who they are. We want a term that neatly categorizes everyone. Socially we cut huge swaths of the populace with the knife of one word: redneck or elitist, liberal or conservative. The list is long. Certainty is seductive and labels add a smarmy sense of security against people not like ourselves. Hear something about someone? Slap a label on them. There. You have them pegged.

But we are complex creatures; our identity is seldom simple and constantly changing. Who am I? In one sense, I'm all the people I've been until now. I've been a bouncing baby boy (so my newspaper birth announcement read) and a pimply teenager. I've been a secret sensualist and a reluctant shift worker. I've been a teacher, student, musician, librarian, philosopher and part-time jerk. All the personas I've been are still inside me, keeping company with who I am now. Who is that?

For starters, I'm the sum of my vast sprawling ancestry which I can now trace to Africa by way of the Genographic Project. I have my mother's thespian bent and my father's quiet patience. To borrow from Buddha, I am a candle lit from a candle lit from a candle. The flame is never the same and never different.

So while none of us is as simple as a single label, I still must ask, for the reasons I'm writing this book, who am I now? What do I now call myself? Freethinker? Naturalist? Humanist? Atheist? Apostate?

Now and then, but more often than I ever realized before, people of faith take a look at what they believe and their thoughts lead them away from their faith. For that they are given the label of "apostate." By dictionary definition, an apostate is simply "a person who renounces a belief or principle." [42] It is a deconversion of sorts. Religion generally doesn't look kindly on those who, shall we say, leave the fold. In some religions, the consequences of apostasy are dire.

Under Islamic law, the penalty for apostasy is death. In other words, if you as a Muslim decide for whatever reason that you no longer hold to the tenets of Islam, you face the penalty of being killed. The Jewish Torah is not all that more sympathetic in theory, though thankfully not in practice. If someone entices someone away from worshipping Yahweh, "*Your hand must be the first in putting him to death, and then the hands of all the people. Stone him to death, because he tried to turn you away from the Lord your God....*" (Deuteronomy 13:9,10).

Thankfully, leaving Christianity does not result in a death sentence. Some say that you can't really leave the faith. Once you are saved, you are always saved. Others say that if you walk out, it's a sign that you never were really in; that is to say that you never really believed deep in your heart. For others, the punishment for apostasy is as dire as for the non-believer who rejects salvation and must bear the wrath of God and forfeit heaven.

For obvious reasons, faith groups don't trumpet their apostates. Sometimes apostates toot their own horn. The *New Yorker* magazine published a profile of Canadian writer-director Paul Haggis' defection from the Church of Scientology simply titled "The Apostate."[43] After months of interviews, staff writer Lawrence Wright described Haggis' experience inside the church and his decision to leave it.

It is tough when someone leaves the tribe. As Haggis admitted in an article in *USA Today*, "I knew it was going to hurt a lot of friends, but you gotta do what you gotta do."[44] Precisely.

Youcef Nadarkhani became a Christian at age 19. He's now 37, married with two children, and is the pastor for a network of Christian house churches in the Iranian city of Rasht. Since Youcef was raised Muslim, and since he left Islam to embrace Christianity, he is now an apostate. Pastor Nadarkani was sentenced to be executed by hanging. An international outcry led to his acquittal.

As I mentioned, the price for Christian apostasy is mild in comparison. If, say, you are no longer a Roman Catholic, you can be excommunicated or formally excluded from participating in the sacraments of the Church. If an Anglican becomes an atheist, they might get funny looks if they appear at the annual roast beef dinner in the parish hall.

Thinking of each religion's sanctions for apostasy, I have one question that still haunts me. What does it say about an organization, or movement, or religion for that matter, which decrees if a member has changed his mind and no longer thinks what he used to think and leaves the group, that he should be shunned or worse, killed? The apostate has not injured anyone or stolen anything. He has not defaced someone's property or demeaned someone's reputation. His only offence is, to borrow from George Orwell's 1984 terminology, *thoughtcrime*.[45]

The offended deity may be insulted or sad that someone is no longer a faithful follower, but why take revenge? What kind of deity would want believers to kill someone who, for whatever reason, no long embraces them? Is God's power somehow diminished by one less person's devotion?

According to Pew Research analysis, one in ten countries in the world outlaw apostasy.[46] The legal punishments vary from fines to death. No one has been executed for apostasy in Iran for more than 20 years, but it behooves all people of any or no faith to protest a provision in any alleged holy book that mandates a death sentence to someone whose only crime was that she changed her mind.

As you might well imagine, once I was thoroughly engaged in this journey from the faith I had espoused, I was drawn to the examples of others who had left their faith: Paul Haggis and Scientology, Somali-born activist Ayaan Hirsi Ali and Islam. How about Christian apostates?

After 19 years as a soul-winning fundamentalist preacher, Dan Barker lost faith in faith and is now the co-president of the *Freedom from Religion Foundation*. Saturday Night Live alumna Julia Sweeney has turned the departure from her Roman Catholic faith into a funny but touching monologue called *Letting Go of God*.

Whether or not you agree with them, if people have thought about the beliefs they embraced or a church they joined, and decided that the precepts no longer hold water or that church membership is unconscionable, they must be free to walk away without being ostracized by family or friends, or facing threats from those angry at the defection.

Other than the negative publicity generated by a celebrity apostate like Haggis or the reduction of income suffered by the local parish that loses a generous giver, why should those remaining in the flock be angered by one who internally and privately changes his/her mind and leaves? This person has not damaged anything or harmed anyone. For that matter, any deity who is so unbelievably insecure as to be insulted or threatened by a solitary soul who no longer believes in him is hardly a proper object of adoration.

While the risks to apostates are many, the reward is that they are being honest with themselves, even if others are mystified by their cynicism. Belief, after all, is not something you can fake or should fake. While God may be sad to lose a believer to disbelief, surely God would prefer honest skepticism to bogus piety. Both shepherd and sheep may lament the loss of one of their flock. But surely if God is just and fair, it is that little lamb's right, if it changes its mind, to leave without being slaughtered.

If you are a person of faith and have read this far, you may be feeling sad. I understand. I understand that no one in any church would relish news that a person of God struggles with belief in God. After her death, Mother Theresa's dark letters emerged. In 1979, for instance, she wrote to Rev. Michael van der Peet, *"Jesus has a very special love for you. As for me, the silence and the emptiness is so great that I look and do not see, listen and do not hear."* [47] She had wanted all her letters destroyed, but the Vatican ordered they be preserved as potential relics of a saint, warts and all.

I have been asked if there are other clergy who have lost their faith but who have kept their silence and their job. No one knows, of course. There are no statistics. Closeted clergy can't be counted. The numbers are a mystery because most are still in the closet, so to speak, about their loss of faith, and are desperately going through the motions for reasons of family and finance. I can tell you, however, that the number is significant. Some time ago I joined the Clergy Project,[48] a confidential online community for active and former clergy who do not hold supernatural beliefs. Many clergy struggle in a web of concealment trying to figure out how to preach a gospel they no longer believe or have redefined beyond recognition.

You may be quick to judge clergy who used to believe. It's easy to say that they should just quit and do something else. I would only advocate for compassion because many of the stories break my heart. Having had a change of heart, why have these clergy stayed in the pulpit? For some, it is to work for social justice or simply help people. Some don't want to rock the boat. Yes, some work for the pay cheque because they have young families and mortgages and are, frankly, afraid and unsure of employment outside the vocation they have studied and trained to pursue.

For those in religious authority who have pondered the age and span of the cosmos, the elegant simplicity of evolution by natural selection, the violence and corruption in church history, the enigma of expiation for sin by blood sacrifice, the discrepancies in scripture, the antagonisms and animosities derived from religious fervour, and decided they can no longer promote the grand scheme of Christianity, what are their options? Stay and cross their fingers? Leave and do something else? What about the family and the mortgage? It's not an easy place. My crisis of faith came in my mid-50s, which allowed me to take early retirement to maintain a sense of integrity. I have been asked how long before I retired did I no longer believe. The answer is not easy. This has been a journey of discovery for me. Once I realized that, as I explained at the time of my retirement, the "fire in my belly had gone out", I knew I needed to stop preaching. While some may accuse me of hypocrisy in those final months, I can only say that my journey from faith to reason had begun, but I couldn't name it as such at the time and I had no idea where it would lead.

There's a fascinating essay in the journal *Evolutionary Psychology* entitled *"Preachers who are not Believers"*.[49] Scientist/philosopher Daniel Dennett and social worker Linda LaScola found five active clergy who were nonbelievers and who agreed to be interviewed in confidence. Their frankness is bracing. All five pastors were grateful for the chance to talk candidly about their refined unbelief with someone who would challenge and probe them without judging them.

With his 1996 novel *In the Beauty of the Lilies*, John Updike tells the story of the Wilmot family, which begins around 1910 when Clarence Wilmot, a Presbyterian minister, realizes he no longer believes in God. Theological books were "paper shields against the molten iron of natural truth."[50] His loss of faith was a palpable event and his life was shattered by his decision to renounce the pulpit.

The tale is fictitious but what should we say to the Clarences? You're going to burn in hell? You should stay in the ministry and do good? Are these clergy the tip of an iceberg? No one knows. Unlike a policy of "don't ask, don't tell", wouldn't it be better if we could ask anyone any question and hear any answer, however unsatisfactory or unsettling, without judgment or threat of being an apostate?

I am well aware that I enjoyed a secure career and steady income based on propositions I now reject. In politics I'd be called a flip-flopper. All I can say is that once I believed with my whole being in the precepts of Christianity and worked tirelessly to promote them and to give myself to those entrusted to my pastoral care. And now my mind has changed. Have you changed your mind about anything, say moral issues such as same sex marriage or capital punishment? How about a political affiliation? My change of mind happened in the arena of religion.

So I guess I am an apostate—one who used to believe and no longer believes. What about those who have never believed and don't believe now? They can't be apostates because they never left a belief system. So what is the best word to describe those who, regardless of what they used to believe or not, do not now believe in a supernatural deity?

Some have adopted the term *freethinker or naturalist*. Freethought emerged in the 17th century as a philosophical view that opinions should be formed on the basis of logic and reason instead of authority and tradition. The term "naturalist" here does not mean someone who collects butterflies but one who considers the universe to be a natural realm with observable laws on which you can make reasonable predictions.

The label I cannot escape, however, is "atheist". I'm uncomfortable with the term not because of its etymology, but its connotations.

Most people believe in (a) god. Others obviously don't. Those who believe cite everything from an amorphous cosmic force to the more personal Yahweh or an incarnation as Jesus Christ. We have different words to describe faith in a god. Pantheists, for instance, believe that the universe and nature itself is a manifestation of god and so god is not personal.

Deists, on the other hand, believe in a supreme being who created everything but who does not intervene in human affairs.

Others believe in a god who not only set the universe in motion but has spoken definitively and continues to intervene in the affairs of humanity. We call them theists.

Those who take the position that there are no deities are atheists. While not naming them, the Bible alludes to atheists: Psalm 10:4 says, *"The wicked, in the haughtiness of his countenance, does not seek Him. All his thoughts are, 'There is no God.'"*

The Greek word "atheos" dates from the seventh century BCE and was later incorporated into Latin. It was an expression of censure levelled at those who not only did not believe in God but also those who did not worship the dominant deity of the day. Rome regarded early Christians as atheists because Christians rejected Rome's gods and refused to bow to them. You could believe in a foreign god and still be condemned as an atheist.

However, the very structure of the word 'a-theist' employs the exclusionary prefix which suggests antagonism. It is therefore used as a pejorative, carrying the connotations of the appalled reaction of believers toward those who abjure belief in the supernatural, meaning, of course, belief in the particular god they worship.

Atheism, then, has over time become an epithet to label and castigate those who believe differently; those who must, therefore, be immoral and unclean and who are somehow intent on waging war on the faith.

I can't help pointing out once again that everyone is an atheist about other people's gods. A Christian does not believe in Thor or Zeus. A Christian rejects all gods except the God as revealed in Jesus of Nazareth. As Richard Dawkins so often points out, an atheist also does not believe in Thor or Zeus, say, but goes one more step and adds to the list the God as revealed in Jesus of Nazareth.

Atheism, then, is not an organized movement. It has no doctrine or structure. It certainly isn't a religion. As pointed out by magician and entertainer Penn Jillette, some people collect stamps and some don't but we don't create a word for people who don't collect stamps. We don't come up with the term "astampers". Those of us who don't believe in fairies are not "afairyists". If atheism is a religion, then bald is a hair colour and "off" is a television channel.

For years, I subscribed to the popular phobia toward atheists. Clearly they were mildly aggressive, amoral souls who needed a saviour. But in my pilgrimage from the pulpit, I have become baffled by the level of hostility theists hold for atheists as if to suggest that if you choose not to believe what I believe, you are somehow suspect. That, by the way, would include people such as Mark Twain, Thomas Edison, Marie Curie, Katharine Hepburn, Bill Gates and Dame Helen Mirren.

In 1999, a Gallup poll asked Americans whether, if they were voting for president, they would vote for a well-qualified person who was female (95 per cent said yes), black (92 per cent), homosexual (79 per cent). Only 45 per cent said they would vote for an atheist.

A joint study out of the University of British Columbia and the University of Oregon, conducted among 350 Americans adults and 420 Canadian college students and published online in *The Journal of Personality and Social Psychology*, suggests the antipathy for atheists has not diminished in the last decade. The researchers found that religious believers thought descriptions of untrustworthy people, those who steal or cheat, were more likely to be atheists than Christians, Muslims, Jews, gays or feminists. The only group they distrusted more than atheists was rapists. The study asked participants to decide if a fictional driver damaged a parked car and left the scene, then found a wallet and took the money, was the driver more likely to be a teacher, an atheist teacher or a rapist teacher? The participants, who were from religious and nonreligious backgrounds, most often chose the atheist teacher.

What's going on here? What drives people of faith to paroxysms of antagonism against those who don't share their faith—a group that is difficult to identify, not organized and certainly not socially powerful? Why do theists consider atheists to be so morally corrupt?

We all tend to be more comfortable with those who think the way we think but it is ludicrous that umbrage should be as intense and pervasive as to conclude that if you don't share my faith, you can't be trusted. I suspect many atheists keep their thoughts to themselves because they don't want to hurt or upset people they care about. They may also be wary of the prejudice of believers toward those who don't share their beliefs.

Some people complain that atheists are arrogant, all unholier than thou. Just like theists, some atheists are nice people and some aren't. Some are fascinating, kind, wonderful people. Of the not-so-nice group, some atheists are smug and proselytizing. They mock religion aggressively and mercilessly and in a way that demeans the personality of the believer as much as the structure of beliefs to which the believer subscribes. Just as Christians, for instance, say you should love the sinner and hate the sin, it is entirely possible, and laudable, for an atheist to love a believer even if you hate what religion does to them.

Believers, too, are prone to confuse passion with arrogance. I now find myself getting passionate when talking about the reasons for my deconversion but at the same time quite open to hearing good counterarguments, other than "... cause the Bible says so!"

So are atheists arrogant? No more than anyone I suppose. What seems particularly arrogant to me is the scenario that someone created an indescribably massive universe teeming with galaxies with a near infinite amount of space between them, and living on one tiny blue planet in the backwoods of one of these massive galaxies is a species of life who think that the whole thing was made for them and that the Creator has a special plan for them. That, I must say, sounds arrogant.

We have very little to be arrogant about. Our history is tainted with delusions of significance, nourished by the assumption that we humans are more important than anything else. Yet with each discovery about the universe, our sense of significance has been eroded. Earth was once assumed to be the centre of everything until we learned that we're just another planet orbiting our sun. We presumed the sun was somehow unique until we learned that the countless stars in the sky are also suns. We presumed our galaxy was the entire universe until we learned that all those fuzzy things in the night sky are actually other galaxies.

So how has my mind changed towards atheists? We, of all people, have every reason to be kind and joyous and enthusiastic. We should live to make the most and the best of this life, since this is all we have. Not only are we not fearful of a hell, but we do not fritter away this life with the death-wish that longs for another life. We live by the truth of the poet Emily Dickinson who wrote, "That it will never come again is what makes life sweet." [51]

Am I an apostate? Yes. Am I an atheist? Yes. The labels are apt. If that upsets believers, I'm sad. I don't want to distress those who have only known me as a pastor but it is important to speak openly about this personal journey. At the same time, I don't want to be seen as religion's fevered antagonist.

I now believe that taken literally, many religious claims are at best unjustified and at worst absurd or repugnant. I recoil at the animosities engendered by religion. I once was driven by the fervour that everyone should have my experience and understanding of the Christian life. Now I reject the very notion that any person or any god has the right to impose rules and morals simply because they say they do.

I feel that for all the good that has come to the world by way of religious devotion, the net effect is negative. Still, the idea that there is simply nothing worthwhile in religion is as absurd as the idea that there is nothing worthwhile in poetry, art, philosophy or science. There are deep human needs at the heart of religion, hungers that have been sated by belief.

It may sound odd, even disingenuous, but I'm grateful for my path to conversion. I'm grateful to my parents who took me to church and for the church itself; for the architecture, both simple and sumptuous; for the music and liturgy; for the wonderfully warm experiences of choir, Sunday School, Wolf Cubs and Boy Scouts. I'm grateful for the wonderful friends I've made along the way, some who remain, with whom I sang and studied. I'm grateful for the wonderful people I served, and served with over the years: dedicated souls who welcomed refugees and fed the hungry; who baked pies and made calls and who did it all so cheerfully. I'm grateful for the freedom in my work to explore and experiment. Not everyone has the opportunities I have enjoyed.

In short, my life has been enriched and nurtured by Christian faith: Christmas, Lenten devotions, Easter, Thanksgiving, singing hymns with others, gazing through stained glass windows, admiring Gothic and Romanesque architecture, funerals, baptisms, candles, sermons, icons, art, drama.

What is life like beyond belief? Where is a non-believer to turn for those things that enrich the lives of believers? Where can you find the same sense of a supporting community if being part of a church or mosque or synagogue is the last thing on your mind? Is there a secular equivalent of a Passover meal or Holy Communion? A dinner party with a theme, perhaps? I am indebted to Alain de Botton who, with deep respect and total impiety, believes that while religion is not true in the God-given sense, the rituals, edifices and art of religion have much to teach us. There is no shame for the secularist to honour religious traditions. As de Botton puts it, "For someone devoid of religious belief, it may be no more of a crime to borrow from a number of faiths than it is for a lover of literature to single out a handful of favourite writers from across the canon." [52]

Christianity gladly appropriated customs and imagery and even dates from pagan practices to advance and extol its understanding of life, so non-believers should have no compunction about taking what is good in religious observances and subsuming them into new customs and practices.

If you love the sound of a pipe organ, you can go to an organ recital. I love choral music. As I write this on my computer, I'm listening to the Tallis Singers perform *Spem in alium* (Latin for "Hope in any other") a 16th century Renaissance motet which, I'm told, is featured in *Fifty Shades of Grey The Classical Album.*

Instead of a patron saint, are there role models for your life? Learn all you can about them. If they are still alive, connect with them somehow. If you were once part of a small group ministry, there are book clubs and discussion groups galore who would welcome new members. If you used to enjoy sitting and listening to a sermon, there are people giving lectures all the time. I particularly enjoy Ted Talks, 20-minute lectures on all kinds of topics.

Some of the art and music that the world counts among the loveliest have been inspired by faith. You can't understand history without understanding what people believed or feared or hoped through their religious world view. Is it possible to have art and music and sport, inspiration and a positive outlook on life unimpeded by the ancient mythologies and superstitions of our Iron Age ancestors? Of course it is.

I love life. I love my life. The chances of my never having been here are far greater than the chance of being here. Six hundred years ago, about six million couples coupled so that I would be here now. In other words, I won the lottery of life. So did you. And if you look at all the life around you, not just the people but the plants and other animals, how can you find joy in shortening life? Other than satisfying my biological need for food, why kill for sport?

To those who might have met me or read my columns for years, let me assure you of something vital. I have not changed. I am the same Bob Ripley as the choirboy, server, guitarist, preacher, lover and friend. I just started to ask questions and listen to answers; to probe and to think. Consistency with my former beliefs was simply no longer possible. I find comfort and courage in my favourite quote from Ralph Waldo Emerson's essay *Self-Reliance.* He wrote, *"A foolish consistency is the hobgoblin of little minds adored by little statesmen and philosophers and divines. With consistency a great soul has simply nothing to do. He may as well concern himself with his shadow on the wall."* [53]

I expressed in the preface that it might be easier to keep this story secret, lest people think less of me and tell me so. No one wants to be shunned by friends or family or even strangers. To those who might know me personally, I hope this isn't goodbye. I hope you'll realize the person you know me to be is exactly the person I am now, warts and all, still striving for integrity and capable of great love.

If you are so inclined to pray for me, may I humbly suggest you take the time you would have spent in prayer and have lunch with a good friend or write an email to someone you love.

You see, I'm not lost. I've not lost my faith as if it were something I accidentally misplaced. I deliberately began this journey by asking questions and continued by not being content with trite clichés or lazy affirmations. Answers can be our idols. Those who carry answers around, ready to dispense them at a moment's notice, forfeit the power of questions. As Jesus of Nazareth may have said, "Blessed are the poor in spirit" (Matthew 5:3) or in my personal paraphrase of that verse, "Blessed are those who don't know it all." Rainer Maria Rilke said, "Be patient toward all that is unresolved in your heart and try to love the questions themselves." [54]

Where my search for answers has led me to a different conclusion than before, rest assured that it has been done thoughtfully and analytically. I continue to be a passionate advocate for unremitting intellectual honesty, for reason and reality, for love and learning. My advocacy simply no longer assumes a deity. I'm thankful that I live at a time in history and in a culture of tolerance where I can say that without fearing I would be burned at the stake or, in some parts of the world today, executed by beheading or stoning.

I still believe. I believe that no person or group of persons is inferior to any other. I believe that what matters is not so much what we believe, but how we conduct ourselves for these few short, fragile years of being alive. I believe that experiencing the beauty and wonder of the universe, including this pale blue dot in the remote corner of our galaxy, is an indescribably wonderful privilege.

I believe in the taste of a cold martini, the smell of a rhubarb pie, the joy of running, the feel of being hugged and so many things that I know exist that make this life the best life I will ever have.

[42] Oxford Concise English Dictionary; Tenth Edition (Revised); 2001; p.62

[43] http://www.newyorker.com/reporting/2011/02/14/110214fa_fact_wright

[44] http://usatoday30.usatoday.com/life/people/2011-02-24-haggis_vanityfair_ST_N.htm

[45] The term was popularized in the novel *Nineteen Eighty Four* Thoughtcrime is the criminal act of holding unspoken beliefs or doubts that oppose or question the ruling party. In the book, the government attempts to control not only the speech and actions, but also the thoughts of its subjects.

[46] http://www.pewresearch.org/fact-tank/2014/05/28/which-countries-still-outlaw-apostasy-and-blasphemy/

[47] http://www.time.com/time/magazine/article/0,9171,1655720,00.html

[48] http://www.clergyproject.org

[49] http://www.epjournal.net/wp-content/uploads/EP08122150.pdf

[50] John Updike, *In the Beauty of the Lilies*, 1st ed. (Franklin Center, Pa.: Franklin Library, 1996), 332.

[51] From the poem *"That It May Never Come Again"* by Emily Dickinson

[52] Alain De Botton, *Religion for Atheists : A Non-Believer's Guide to the Uses of Religion*, 1st U.S. ed. (New York: Pantheon Books, 2012), 17.

[53] Emerson et al., 145-146.

[54] Rainer Maria Rilke and M. D. Herter Norton, *Letters to a Young Poet [by] Rainer Maria Rilke, Translation by M.D. Herter Norton* (New York,: W.W. Norton & company, 1934). Letter Three (April 23, 1903)

· BIBLIOGRAPHY ·

Aslan, Reza. *Zealot : The Life and Times of Jesus of Nazareth*. First Edition. ed. New York: Random House, 2013.

Bock, Fred. *The Late Great Planet Earth Song Book*. 1 vols. Grand Rapids, Mich.: Singspiration Music, 1973.

Buechner, Frederick. *Wishful Thinking : A Seeker's Abc*. Rev. and expanded ed. San Francisco, Calif.: HarperSanFrancisco, 1993.

Darwin, Charles. *On the Origin of Species, 1859 The Works of Charles Darwin*. Washington Square, N.Y.: New York University Press, 1988.

Dawkins, Richard. *Unweaving the Rainbow: Science, Delusion, and the Appetite for Wonder*. Boston: Houghton Mifflin, 1998.

Dawkins, Richard. *The Ancestor's Tale: A Pilgrimage to the Dawn of Evolution*. Boston: Houghton Mifflin, 2004.

Dawkins, Richard. *The Selfish Gene*. 30th anniversary ed. Oxford; New York: Oxford University Press, 2006.

Dawkins, Richard. *The God Delusion*. 1st Mariner Books ed. Boston: Houghton Mifflin Co., 2008.

Dawkins, Richard. *The Greatest Show on Earth: The Evidence for Evolution*. 1st Free Press hardcover ed. New York: Free Press, 2009.

Dawkins, Richard and Dave McKean. *The Magic of Reality: How We Know What's Really True.* 1st Free Press hardcover ed. New York: Free Press, 2011.

De Botton, Alain. *Religion for Atheists: A Non-Believer's Guide to the Uses of Religion.* 1st U.S. ed. New York: Pantheon Books, 2012.

Dennett, Daniel Clement. *Breaking the Spell: Religion as a Natural Phenomenon.* New York: Viking, 2006.

Ehrman, Bart D. *Jesus, Apocalyptic Prophet of the New Millennium.* Oxford ; New York: Oxford University Press, 1999.

Ehrman, Bart D. *Lost Christianities: The Battle for Scripture and the Faiths We Never Knew.* New York: Oxford University Press, 2003.

Ehrman, Bart D. *Lost Scriptures: Books That Did Not Make It into the New Testament.* New York: Oxford University Press, 2003.

Ehrman, Bart D. *Misquoting Jesus: The Story Behind Who Changed the Bible and Why.* 1st ed. New York: HarperSanFrancisco, 2005.

Ehrman, Bart D. *Peter, Paul, and Mary Magdalene: The Followers of Jesus in History and Legend.* Oxford ; New York: Oxford University Press, 2006.

Ehrman, Bart D. *God's Problem: How the Bible Fails to Answer Our Most Important Question—Why We Suffer.* 1st ed. New York: HarperOne, 2008.

Ehrman, Bart D. *Jesus, Interrupted: Revealing the Hidden Contradictions in the Bible (and Why We Don't Know About Them).* 1st ed. New York: HarperOne, 2009.

Ehrman, Bart D. F*orged: Writing in the Name of God: Why the Bible's Authors Are Not Who We Think They Are.* 1st ed. New York: HarperOne, 2011.

Ehrman, Bart D. *Did Jesus Exist?: The Historical Argument for Jesus of Nazareth.* 1st ed. New York: HarperOne, 2012.

Emerson, Ralph Waldo, Carl Bode and Malcolm Cowley. *The Portable Emerson.* Rev. ed. The Viking Portable Library. New York: Penguin, 1981.

Ertz, Susan. *Anger in the Sky.* New York and London: Harper & Brothers, 1943.

Grayling, A. C. *The God Argument: The Case against Religion and for Humanism.* New York, Bloomsbury USA, 2013.

Grayling, A. C. *The Good Book: A Secular Bible.* Walker Publishing Co, Inc., New York, 2011.

Grayling, A. C. *Ideas That Matter: The Concepts That Shape the 21st Century.* New York: Basic Books, 2010.

Guirand, Felix. *New Larousse Encyclopedia of Mythology.* New ed. London, New York: Hamlyn, 1968.

Harpur, Tom. *The Pagan Christ: Recovering the Lost Light.* New York: Walker & Co., 2005.

Harris, Sam. *The End of Faith: Religion, Terror, and the Future of Reason.* 1st ed. New York: W.W. Norton & Co., 2004.

Harris, Sam. *Letter to a Christian Nation.* 1st Vintage Books ed. New York: Vintage Books, 2008.

Harris, Sam. *The Moral Landscape: How Science Can Determine Human Values.*
1st Free Press hardcover ed. New York: Free Press, 2010.

Harris, Sam. *Free Will.* 1st Free Press trade paperback ed. New York: Free Press,
2012.

Hitchens, Christopher. *God Is Not Great : How Religion Poisons Everything.*
1st ed. New York: Twelve, 2007.

Hitchens, Christopher. *The Portable Atheist: Essential Readings for the
Nonbeliever.* 3rd Da Capo Press ed. Philadelphia, Penn: Da Capo, 2007.

Loftus, John W. *Why I Became an Atheist: A Former Preacher Rejects Christianity.*
Rev. and expanded ed. Amherst, N.Y.: Prometheus Books, 2012.

Meredith, George. *Modern Love, and Other Poems.* Old World Series 12.
Portland, Me.,: T. B. Mosher, 1898.

Miles, Jack. *Christ: A Crisis in the Life of God.* 1st ed. New York: Alfred A.
Knopf, 2001.

Mills, David and Dorion Sagan. *Atheist Universe: The Thinking Person's Answer
to Christian Fundamentalism.* Berkeley, Calif.: Ulysses Press, 2006.

Norwich, John Julius. *Absolute Monarchs: A History of the Papacy.* 1st U.S. ed.
New York: Random House, 2011.

Pagels, Elaine H. *Beyond Belief: The Secret Gospel of Thomas.* 1st ed. New York:
Random House, 2003.

Paulos, John Allen. *Irreligion: A Mathematician Explains Why the Arguments for
God Just Don't Add Up.* 1st ed. New York: Hill and Wang, 2008.

Pinker, Steven. *How the Mind Works.* New York: Norton, 1997.

Rilke, Rainer Maria and M. D. Herter Norton. *Letters to a Young Poet [by] Rainer Maria Rilke, Translation by M.D. Herter Norton.* New York,: W.W. Norton & Company, 1934.

Russell, Bertrand. *Religion and Science.* New York: H. Holt, 1935.

Russell, Bertrand and Rouben Mamoulian Collection (Library of Congress). *Why I Am Not a Christian, and Other Essays on Religion and Related Subjects.* New York: Simon and Schuster, 1957.

Sagan, Carl. *Pale Blue Dot: A Vision of the Human Future in Space.* 1st ed. New York: Random House, 1994.

Shermer, Michael. *The Believing Brain: From Ghosts and Gods to Politics and Conspiracies—How We Construct Beliefs and Reinforce Them as Truths.* 1st ed. New York: Times Books, 2011.

Stenger, Victor J. *The New Atheism: Taking a Stand for Science and Reason.* Amherst, N.Y.: Prometheus Books, 2009.

Updike, John. *In the Beauty of the Lilies.* 1st ed. Franklin Center, Penn.: Franklin Library, 1996.

Wesley, John, Percy Livingstone Parker and Augustine Birrell. *The Heart of John Wesley's Journal.* New York,: Fleming H. Revell Co., 1903.